LITTLE BOOK OF THE
SPITFIRE

Written by **David Curnock**

LITTLE BOOK OF THE
SPITFIRE

This edition first published in the UK in 2009
By Green Umbrella Publishing

© Green Umbrella Publishing 2009

www.gupublishing.co.uk

Publishers Jules Gammond and Vanessa Gardner

Printed and bound in China

ISBN: 978-1-906635-58-9

The views in this book are those of the author but they are general views
only and readers are urged to consult the relevant and qualified specialist for
individual advice in particular situations.

Green Umbrella Publishing hereby exclude all liability to the extent permitted
by law of any errors or omissions in this book and for any loss, damage or
expense (whether direct or indirect) suffered by a third party relying on any
information contained in this book.

All our best endeavours have been made to secure copyright clearance
for every photograph used but in the event of any copyright owner being
overlooked please address correspondence to Green Umbrella Publishing
The Old Bakehouse, 21 The Street, Lydiard Millicent, Swindon SN5 3LU

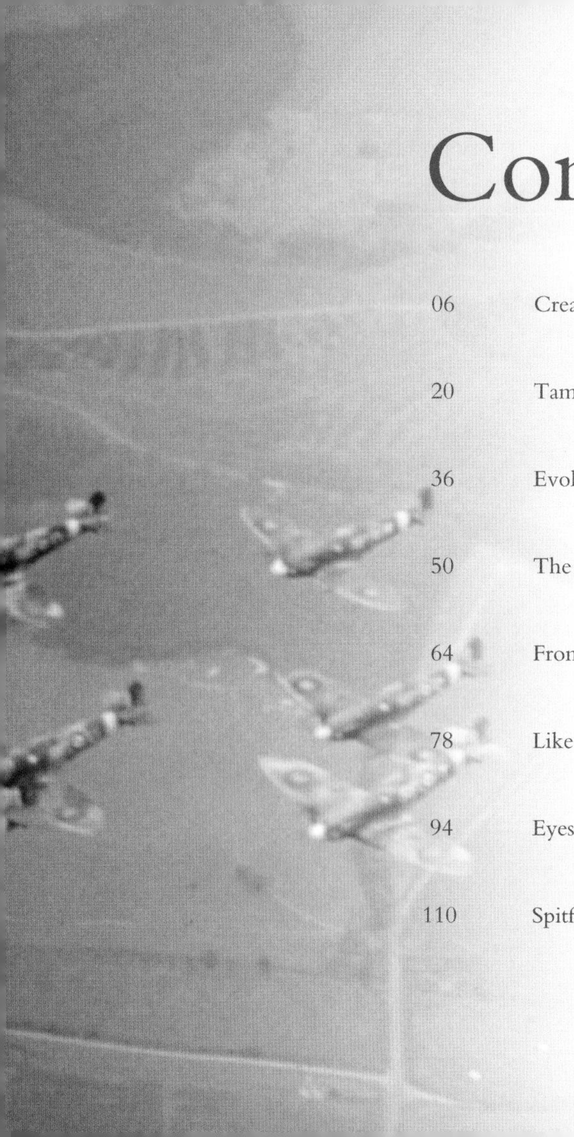

Contents

06   Creator of a Legend

20   Taming the Shrew

36   Evolution of an Icon

50   The Power and the Growler

64   From the Cockpit

78   Like a Duck to Water

94   Eyes in the Skies

110   Spitfire Notes and Anecdotes

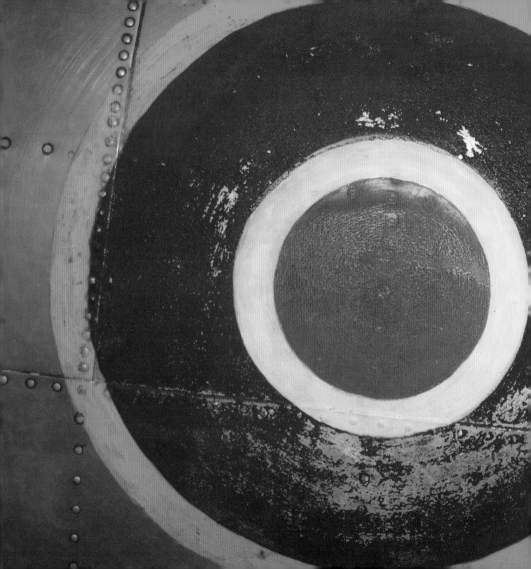

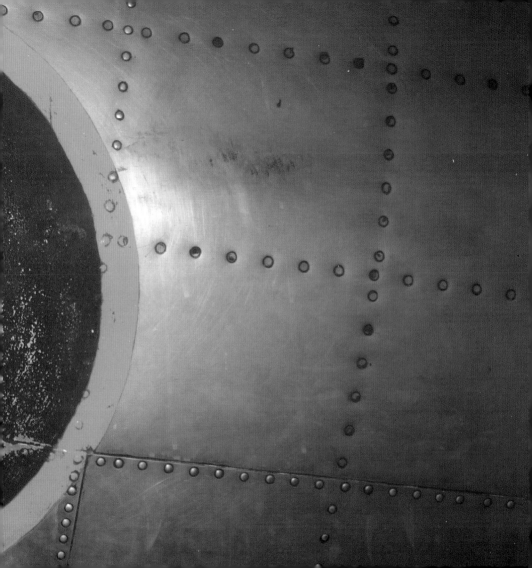

Creator of a Legend

"If anybody ever tells you anything about an aeroplane which is so bloody complicated you can't understand it, take it from me: it's all balls." – R J Mitchell

Reginald Joseph Mitchell was born on 20 May 1895 at 115 Congleton Road, Butt Lane, Stoke-on-Trent, the eldest of three sons. His parents, Herbert and Eliza Mitchell, were both teachers, which may have accounted for his academic leanings and abilities. His father had been headmaster at several local schools before starting his own printing business. It was at Hanley High School where the young Reginald first showed his almost obsessional interest in aviation; designing, building, and flying model aeroplanes.

However, his working life took him in a different direction when, as a 16-year-old, he began an apprenticeship at the locomotive engine works of Kerr Stuart and Co, in Stoke. Beginning in the engine workshop, he progressed to the drawing office. Known in those days as "night school", he attended evening classes where he studied mechanics, engineering drawing, and higher mathematics. After completing his apprenticeship in 1917, he applied for a job as assistant to Hubert Scott-Paine, the owner and chief designer of Pemberton Billing Ltd, later to become the Supermarine Aviation Works, at Woolston, near Southampton. Mitchell was offered the post and such was his enthusiasm to get started, he sent for his belongings rather than go back to Staffordshire to collect them.

By 1918, he had been promoted to the post of assistant works manager and, in the same year, he married his wife Florence Dayson, a woman 10 years his senior. She was a headmistress whom he had met, and courted, in the Midlands before his relocation to the Southampton area. At the age of only 24, Mitchell was appointed chief designer and, a year later, was made chief engineer. His technical brilliance led to his meteoric rise within the company, and was also recognised with the award of a 10 year contract of employment: this was followed by his being given a technical directorship in 1927. He was so important to the company that, in 1928, when Vickers took over the Supermarine company, it was a condition of the takeover agreement that Mitchell be contractually bound to serve with them, for a period of five years, until 1935. Even though he was not a well man, having been diagnosed with cancer in 1933, he refused to give up his work and remained with the company right up to his untimely death, two years beyond that contractual stipulation.

Mitchell was responsible for the design and development of Supermarine's range of flying boats and was personally involved in the design of more than 20 of these types.

His association with the creation of aircraft such as the Sea Eagle, Scarab and, particularly, the Southampton, helped the Supermarine factory become both profitable and well-known throughout the aviation world. The Southampton was an armed development of the Swan and was ordered directly off the drawing board, by the Air Ministry, in 1924. It proved successful and went on to equip six squadrons in the RAF, remaining in service until 1936. Other Mitchell-designed successes included the Walrus amphibian, and the Stranraer flying boat, the latter being his last boat-hulled design.

Although his work on flying boats was, in itself, an important contribution in the realm of British aviation achievements, he became even better known for his prowess in the world of high-speed flight and, particularly, his involvement in the Schneider Trophy air races. His refinement of the Supermarine Baby, a small biplane flying boat, resulted in the Sea Lion II: this aircraft proved victorious in the 1922 Schneider Trophy, thereby denying the Italians an outright third win, as they had already won the previous two events. The Sea Lion II, flown by Henri

◀ The Supermarine Sea Lion III during preparations for the Schneider Trophy race in 1923.

▶ Flt Lt D'Arcy Greig in his Supermarine S5 N219 in which he attempted to break the world air speed record.

Biard, won at an average speed of 145.72mph.

The success of the Americans in the 1923 races at Cowes, Isle of Wight, was food for thought for R J Mitchell. He had long been an admirer of the designs of Glenn Curtiss, an American who specialised in water-borne aircraft. The Blackburn Pellet, and the Supermarine Sea Lion III had been chosen to defend the trophy on behalf of the host country. The Pellet sank during the sea navigability section of the competition, leaving the Sea Lion to compete as the sole British representative. Ultimately, it finished third, behind two Curtiss CR3s from the USA. The winning aircraft, flown by US Navy Lt David Rittenhouse, averaged 177.39mph, more than 26mph faster than Mitchell's design: this massive speed differential caused the Briton to rethink his design strategy.

Hitherto, the Supermarine designs

aerial progress. The winning Curtiss CR3, and its compatriot the Wright NW2 (which sank during the same 1923 event), were also biplanes but with the major difference that they were float-planes, each having a slender fuselage, strut-mounted above twin floats. They also differed in the placement of the engine and propeller: the Supermarine design featured a pusher propeller driven by a non-cowled Napier Lion engine that was mounted below the upper wing, and with a large radiator mounted below the front of the wing; the Curtiss CR3 was powered by a closely-cowled engine, fitted in the aircraft's nose, driving a tractor-style propeller. Although both

had all been based on the biplane flying boat principle, with a boat-style hull. While this generally resulted in fairly good sea behaviour, it was not an ideal configuration for high-speed

▶ Engineers testing the engine of a Supermarine S6B.

designs had engines that produced a similar power output, the Curtiss design was visibly "cleaner" and looked much faster than the cluttered appearance of the British-built Sea Lion flying boat.

Mitchell set about designing a new contender, adopting the float-plane principle. His first, unsuccessful attempt to regain the Schneider Trophy for Britain was the Supermarine S4. The designation "S", used to identify this series of high-speed aircraft is often attributed to the company name, Supermarine: however, authoritative sources claim that it relates to "Schneider", as the sole purpose of these aircraft was to enter and, hopefully, win the Schneider Trophy races. The S4 was a slim-fuselage monoplane with twin floats, and was powered by a 700hp Napier Lion engine. Its appearance in the 1925 series, held in the USA, was less than glorious: during a high-speed test flight, the S4 developed aileron flutter and crashed into the waters of Chesapeake Bay, off Baltimore, Maryland. Fortunately, the pilot, Henri Biard, survived the impact. The British challenge was left to the Gloster III, piloted by Hubert Broad, who finished in second place at an average speed of

just over 199mph. The American winner was a Curtiss R2C-2 of the US Army Air Service, piloted by 1st Lt James H Doolittle, at an average speed of 232.573mph.

Lessons learned from the S4 were used to great effect in the S5 programme. By this time, Mitchell had also been granted the twin benefits of the use of the wind tunnel at the Royal Aircraft Establishment, Farnborough, and the marine test tank facility at the National Physical Laboratory. The S4 project itself had not been a total disaster: it was a very advanced design with its cantilever monoplane wing,

a 680hp Napier Lion VII engine, and formed the basis for Mitchell's next challenger, the Supermarine S5, for the 1927 series of races. For this series, in Venice, the Americans had withdrawn, leaving it as a head-to-head contest between Italy and Great Britain. The RAF High Speed Flight represented their country, having been established in May 1927. It had been originally proposed that the Napier Lion engine, now developing 900hp, would be replaced in the S5 by a Rolls-Royce engine: it was, however, decided to keep the Napier engine for the Venice event.

◄ A formation of Spitfires.

▼ A Supermarine S6B outside its hangar.

Three S5s, serial numbers N219, N220 and N221, were built. A radical departure from that of the S4 design was the use of wing bracing wires; this, together with the change from fabric to metal cladding on the ailerons, solved the wing flutter problem that had resulted in the S4 crash at Baltimore. The slim, streamlined fuselage left precious little space for the pilot, let alone for fuel. Mitchell's solution was to use the starboard float to store the fuel, gaining the additional benefits of lowering the centre of gravity and improving stability in flight. Radiators in the wings provided engine cooling. The S5 was triumphant, N220 winning the 1927 event at an average speed of 281.65mph, with N219 finishing second.

By 1929, the Rolls-Royce R engine was producing significantly more horsepower than the Napier, and was selected to power the Supermarine S6 for Britain's defence of the trophy. Mitchell set to and designed the S6 around the new engine. This necessitated the whole of the wing structure, except for the ailerons, being used to contain the engine's liquid coolant, and pipes within corrugated

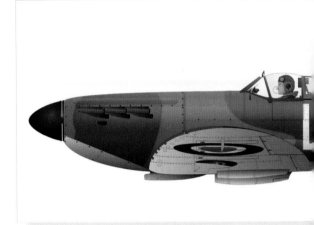

▶ The Spitfire Mark I design benefited from experience gained during the Schneider Trophy series.

fairings along the sides of the fuselage provided the cooling for the engine oil. Because of its importance in helping to keep the engine cool, the S6 was sometimes referred to, by its designer, as "the flying radiator". The floats were also redesigned using data from Mitchell's aerodynamic and hydrodynamic testing. Mitchell's radical design paid off: the Schneider Trophy stayed in Britain, the event being won by S6 serial number N247, flown by Flying Officer H R Waghorn at a speed of 328.63mph, with S6 number N248 in second place, although this aircraft was later disqualified for missing a course marker.

Britain won the Schneider Trophy outright after a third consecutive win in 1931. Mitchell's development of the 1929 aircraft was designated the S6B, and two new airframes were built, serial numbers S1595 and S1596. The two 1929 aircraft were modified to the same standard, and designated S6A. By this time, the R engine was producing over 2,000hp. In the race, S1595 was victorious, at an average speed of 340mph. Later, an S6B set a new world air speed record at 407.5mph. In 1932, Mitchell was awarded the CBE for his contribution towards Britain's achievements in the world of high-speed flight.

In spite of his success in the world of aviation, Mitchell was not particularly well-known outside that sphere of activity, being an intensely private man

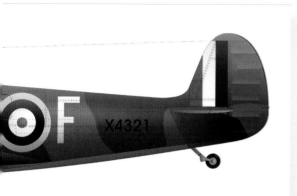

design work on a new bomber project.

The bomber never materialised, as the plans for it, and a wooden mock-up, were lost when German bombs destroyed much of the Supermarine works early in the war. Prior to his death on 11 June 1937, at the age of 42, he had seen the fruits of his labours on the fighter project take to the skies. He did not live to see how important his contribution was to prove, in the dark years of conflict that were soon to follow. In a BBC Midlands television poll in 2003, R J Mitchell was voted the "Greatest Midlander of all Time", beating William Shakespeare into second place. Long after his death, his achievements have been recognised by the erection of a statue in his honour, and civic buildings have been given his name, the citizens of his home town rightfully acknowledging his importance in British aviation history.

who shunned all personal publicity. His personal qualities of kindness and humanity towards those with whom he came into contact, particularly within the Supermarine company, earned the respect and affection of his staff and colleagues. His resolute nature came to the fore in 1933, when he was diagnosed with cancer of the bowel. After a major operation, he refused to give up his work, and continued with his design activities: he was working on the plans for a new fighter aircraft, utilising his experiences in the Schneider Trophy: Mitchell had also started preliminary

Taming the Shrew

If things had turned out differently, the aircraft that became known as the Spitfire could possibly have been named Shrew, or Shrike, as these were among the names proposed by the Air Ministry for their new fighter aircraft. In 1930, they issued a specification for a new day and night fighter, armed with four machine guns: Supermarine were among those companies that were interested in becoming involved in the project; in due course, Mitchell designed the Supermarine Type 224 to meet that specification.

The result was an unlikely-looking, open-cockpit aeroplane of stressed-skin construction, with an inverted gull wing, no wing flaps, and a fixed undercarriage housed in trouser-like fairings. The 660hp Rolls-Royce Goshawk engine gave a design speed of 228mph: engine cooling was by the method used in the

S-series Schneider Trophy aircraft, the leading edges of the gull wing acting as condensers, with the collector tanks for the condensed water being housed in the trouser fairings. Only one prototype was built: a combination of factors resulted in the contract for the fighter being awarded to Gloster for a derivative of the Gauntlet fighter, the Gladiator, which was destined to become the last biplane fighter to be ordered by the RAF.

Much of the criticism of the Type 224 was levelled at the choice of engine. Although the Air Ministry suggested that the most modern engines should

◀ Training getting underway.

be considered in all new-design aircraft, this was never stipulated in the contract. The eventual winner, the Gladiator, and the Bristol Type 133 contender that was later to be lost in an accident, were both powered by a more traditional, air-cooled radial engine, the Bristol Mercury. The Type 224 did not offer a significant performance increase over its rivals; its climb rate was inferior to that of the Gladiator, it was technically more complex, and its flapless configuration gave it a much higher landing speed than its biplane competitor.

Even before the rejection of the Type 224, Mitchell had commenced his next project, the Supermarine Type 300. For this new design, it was intended

► A Battle of Britain type "scramble". An improved Spitfire is pushed onto the runway by a group of pilots from the squadron.

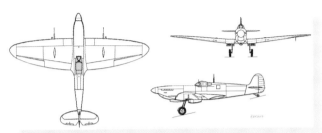

◀ Diagram of a Spitfire Mark XI.

to again use the Goshawk engine, so the wing leading edges were designed to act as condensation tanks for the cooling system. When the Rolls-Royce PV-12 engine, later to be known as the Merlin, became available, it was initially proposed that it should be steam-cooled, so the condensation system was retained, supplemented by a small radiator. Later in the development of the Merlin, the unreliability of the steam cooling system led to this being discarded, being replaced initially by a more efficient pressurised all-liquid, ethylene glycol system, later changed to a water/ ethylene glycol mixture system.

The Air Ministry specification called for a minimum speed, in level flight, of at least 195mph, with a service ceiling of not less than 28,000ft. A further rate of climb stipulation was that the aircraft should reach 15,000ft in eight and a half minutes, or less. No preference for either a biplane or monoplane was specified. Provision was to be made for the carriage of full oxygen and wireless equipment, and the fighter should be capable of day and night operations. With the amended specification taking into account the design features of Mitchell's latest offering, the Type 300 eventually met all the physical requirements: although the design calculations indicated compliance with the specified criteria, the performance could only be demonstrated in flight.

The strengthened wing leading edge was no longer required for cooling purposes; however, it was retained, and formed an integral part of the wing structure. The wing design incorporated a hollow, square-section main spar boom built up from five sections that slotted into each other. Two of these spar

booms were connected by an alloy spar web, the whole spar assembly giving the wing strength and resilience. The leading edge skin was flush riveted, thereby improving air flow and reducing drag; to the rear of the main spar, the top skin was secured by domed rivets. Some parts of the lower skin were originally fixed by wood screws, into spruce sections, but this method was later changed to pop-riveting into metalwork.

The outwards-retracting undercarriage was housed in the thickest part of the wing, immediately to the rear of the main spar. Its narrow track was a compromise between ground handling and wing thickness: the undercarriage attachments fed the landing loads into the strongest part of the wing structure, thereby minimising the need for additional load-bearing structural material, and any consequent increase in weight. The elegant plan form of the wing, incorporated "washout", wherein the angle of attack of the wing progressively reduces towards the wing tips, contributing greatly to a pilot's feel for the aircraft, particularly the onset of stall, thus enabling a tight turning radius to be maintained in aerial combat. The wing also proved capable of good high-speed performance, a factor that was to become apparent in later developments of the Type 300's successors.

It was originally envisaged that four machine guns would be fitted, two in each wing, along with a total of 2,000 rounds of ammunition. This was later changed to satisfy an Air Ministry requirement for six, or eight, machine guns. Mitchell's elliptical wing shape was relatively thin but it proved possible to house four guns and their respective ammunition tanks in each wing. No fuel was carried in the wing at this stage, the single fuel tank being mounted between the engine and the cockpit. The limited capacity for the carriage of fuel had an adverse impact on the aircraft's range that was not overcome until much later in the development of the Spitfire. The placement of the fuel tank was not conducive to the confidence or the well-being of the pilot when in aerial combat. An accurately placed or stray round of ammunition could be disastrous for the pilot if it hit the fuel tank, the ensuing likely conflagration being only inches in front of the unfortunate aviator. Coupled with the close confines of the cockpit, that made entry and egress difficult at best, many

◀ Spitfire MJ730 was known as the "CO's Query" due to its unusual unit code marking.

▶ K5054,
the Spitfire
prototype during
a demonstration
flight at
Eastleigh.

pilots made an adrenaline-fuelled exit through flames and smoke; many were badly burned in the process.

Unlike that of the Hurricane, the fuselage was of monocoque construction, a method that had been proven in the Supermarine S-series of Schneider Trophy fame. The all-metal fuselage was made up from a series of oval-shaped frames, pierced with lightening holes, connected by two main longerons and a series of longitudinal stringers, all covered by a riveted stressed-skin cladding. This arrangement afforded the possibility for the installation of bulky camera equipment in later developments, although its relatively complex method of construction, compared to the tubular frame and fabric-covering of earlier types of fighter, caused problems in both manufacturing and in-service repair.

The Type 300 project was developed by Supermarine as a private venture, although the Air Ministry was aware of its existence: recognition of its potential as a front-line fighter was soon to come in the guise of Specification F10/35. This was written around the new aircraft design, taking into account its range limitations, and was soon followed

LITTLE BOOK OF THE SPITFIRE

by official funding for the building of the prototype. Ably assisted by the aerodynamicist, Beverley Shenstone, and his own familiar and trusted team of detail designers, Mitchell, by now a very sick man, devoted his last few working months to the project.

Construction of the prototype commenced in December 1934. The Air Ministry had allocated the registration K5054 to the first aircraft, probably one of the best-known serial numbers in the history of aviation. They had also suggested a series of possible names for the aircraft: the usual policy was for the model name to begin with the same letter as that of the aircraft manufacturer, hence the list of possibles suggested by the ministry included Shrew, and Shrike. The final name selected by the company, that was now part of the Vickers organisation, is said to have been suggested by Sir Robert McLean, a director, who had often referred to his daughter Ann as being "a little spitfire". The word "spitfire" was in common usage in 16th century Britain, usually in the context of a female with a fiery spirit or temperament. Having previously been used, unofficially, for the Type 224, it was formally approved for

◀ The press taking an interest in K5054, the Spitfire prototype.

► Factory workers at the Supermarine Works in Southampton, drilling parts for the Spitfire.

the new fighter. R J Mitchell's reaction was that it was "just the sort of bloody silly name they would choose".

Visually, the Spitfire was a beautiful and well-proportioned aircraft. With a length of 30ft, wingspan of 37ft and being just over 8ft high, it weighed 5359lb. Its fixed-pitch propeller was driven by a Rolls-Royce Merlin engine that had an output of 990hp. Its clean lines differed markedly from the generation of biplane fighters that were in current front-line service. Apart from its two-bladed propeller, a tail skid instead of a tailwheel, and the lack of undercarriage doors, the prototype would, today, still be instantly recognisable as a Spitfire, had it survived. Keen spotters will note that there was a horizontal horn balance at the top of the rudder, and the cockpit canopy was flush fitting rather than the bulged shape on later versions. Apart from these relatively minor details, the Spitfire's distinctive outline remained largely unchanged throughout much of its lengthy production run. The pace of development was such that there was no time to apply a paint finish prior to the maiden flight. By early March of 1936, the series of ground tests and engine

runs had been completed, and the necessary certification had been signed off by the Aeronautical Inspection Directorate. The Spitfire was ready to take to the skies.

The first flight of the Spitfire prototype K5054 took place at Eastleigh, now known as Southampton Airport,

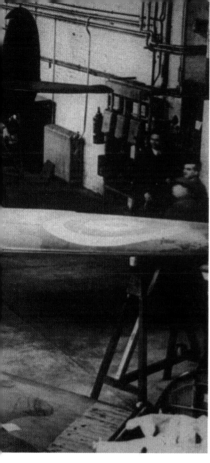

40 different aircraft types in a test-flying career of over 30 years, certainly knew his aeroplanes: after the flight he was reported to have said that it had "handled beautifully" and to the engineers said, "don't touch a thing!", a testament to the design skills of Mitchell and his team. The maiden flight had lasted around eight minutes. In the next few days, Summers carried out further tests, gradually exploring the flight envelope with a series of steep turns and stalls, amassing one hour and 44 minutes of flight time in three days.

Subsequently, the Spitfire achieved a speed of 349mph. Further test flight results proved that this was going to be an outstanding aircraft, and its promise was rewarded by the Air Ministry placing an order for 310 aircraft, on 3 June 1936, even before the test programme had been completed. Over the next few weeks, flight testing continued without major problems and, on 26 May 1936, K5054 was handed over to the Aeroplane and Armament Experimental Establishment at Martlesham Heath for her official trials. Resulting from these trials, minor refinements to the design were made, bringing the prototype up to the

◄ The Spitfire production line at the Vickers Supermarine Works in Southampton.

on 5 March 1936, piloted by Joseph "Mutt" Summers, the Vickers chief test pilot. This vastly experienced pilot, who carried out the first flight of over

▶ A Spitfire about to land.

standard that effectively became the pattern for the first production version. Undercarriage door fairings and a tailwheel in place of the skid were the more obvious visual changes made to the production aircraft.

Things did not run altogether smoothly during the flight trials: on 22 March 1937, the Merlin lost its oil pressure and K5054 was damaged when it made a forced belly landing on open heathland in Suffolk. After repairs, the flight tests continued. The main problems in the flight testing phase centred on the controls, particularly wing flutter at high speeds. Minor changes to the control system, together with the change to the use of an all-metal skin covering for the ailerons instead of the previous fabric, cured this particular defect.

One fateful day followed another: on 3 September 1939, Britain declared

war on Germany; the following day saw K5054 destroyed in a crash at the Royal Aircraft Establishment, Farnborough, when it nosed over on landing. The

such force that it took the Sutton seat harness anchor with it, bending the backrest of the pilot's seat rearwards in the impact. Lesson learned, the seat harness anchor cable was attached to the rear fuselage structure in production aircraft.

However, the gestation period of the Spitfire was almost complete; her baptism of fire was about to take place. The era of the British monoplane piston-engined fighter had begun; few at the time had any idea of the importance of this aircraft, both in military terms, and the uplifting effect on the morale of the British

pilot, Flt Lt White, died of injuries received when the mast that was situated to the rear of the cockpit, was pushed downwards through the fuselage with nation in the dark days of war. Neither did they have any reason to believe that the Spitfire would still be in RAF service for a period of around 15 years.

Evolution of an Icon

The name of R J Mitchell will always be associated with the design of the Spitfire. Unfortunately, he only lived long enough to see his creation take its maiden flight before his untimely death, some 15 months later. The onerous task of developing the Spitfire fell to his chief draughtsman, Joseph "Joe" Smith, who had succeeded Mitchell as chief designer. Smith was responsible for keeping the Spitfire at the cutting edge of Britain's fighter force, his expertise being reflected in the accolade given by an aviation historian who wrote, "If Mitchell was born to design the Spitfire, Joe Smith was born to defend and develop it": this he did to great effect. During its service life, the weight of the Spitfire increased by more than half, its engine power more than doubled, and its top speed rose by between 25 and 30 percent, compared to that of the first version to enter service.

Joseph Smith was reported, on several occasions, as having said at design meetings and elsewhere that "… the good big 'un will eventually beat the good little 'un", with particular reference to aircraft engines. Although the Merlin was an exceptional engine, Smith believed that the Griffon, with its much greater capacity of 36 litres, against the 27 litres of the Merlin, had more potential for development, as the Merlin had been taken almost to the practical limit of its power output. He had wanted the Griffon to be installed in the Spitfire as early as 1940, but the military circumstances, later known as the Battle of Britain, caused this to be deferred until the spring of 1941. Before the end of that year the first Griffon engine, a Griffon IIB with a single-stage

bladed version of the prototype and early production versions, to the contra-rotating, six-bladed installation of the Seafire 47. A series of different wing and armament arrangements, known as the A, B, C, or E wings, were used across the various marks and derivatives. The "A" wing housed eight 0.303in machine guns and lacked the large bulge on the upper surface, distinguishing it from the cannon-equipped types; the "B" wing had four 0.303in machine guns and two 20mm Hispano cannon, the "C" (or commonly, "Universal" wing) could be fitted with either four 20mm cannon or two 20mm cannon and four 0.303in machine guns, and the "E" variation had two 20mm cannon and two 0.50in Browning heavy machine guns. Later in its development, a laminar flow wing was introduced in order to improve high-speed performance, but this development was overtaken by the introduction of the jet fighter into RAF service and did not enter full production.

◀ Joseph Smith, chief designer at Supermarine.

supercharger, was installed in what was basically a modified Spitfire Mark III airframe, now designated as a Spitfire Mark IV, serial number DP845, and made its first flight with Jeffrey Quill at the controls on 27 November 1941, from Worthy Down Aerodrome.

In all, there were 24 distinct marks of Spitfire, and many sub-variants. Differences between marks were largely defined by their engine and propeller, Merlin or Griffon, with propellers ranging from the fixed-pitch, two-

Not all marks of Spitfire were built from scratch: some were converted during build, or from earlier production aircraft, making things somewhat complicated for the uninitiated to

▶ Men working
on the fuselage
of a Spitfire.

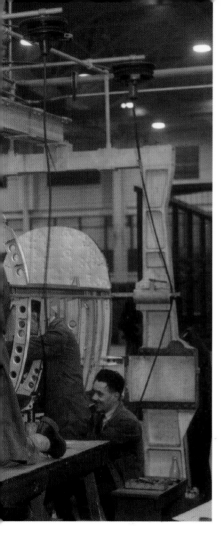

understand. Even the method of numbering the different marks was changed, as the design progressed; earlier versions were numbered in Roman numerals but, from the Mark 21 onwards, the numbers were given in Arabic numerals. Some references to the Marks XVIII and XIX also used Arabic numerals, many eminent Spitfire authorities disagree over which is the correct form. In some cases, a suffix letter was added, usually to signify the wing type variation within that particular mark, and other versions with specialist tasks, such as the photo reconnaissance or fighter reconnaissance Spitfires, were given the prefix PR or FR followed by the mark number.

Type 300-Spitfire Mark I. This was the first production version and entered RAF service with Nos 19 and 66 Squadrons in 1938. With its Merlin II engine giving 1,030hp at 16,250ft, it had an official top speed of 347mph but, with the addition of a bullet-proof windscreen and armour plating for pilot protection, it was probably somewhat slower by around 20mph. Early aircraft had a flush-topped canopy; later deliveries had the bulged, Malcolm-type of bubble canopy. The de Havilland

▶ A Spitfire
Mark I.

three-bladed movable-pitch propeller replaced the original fixed-pitch unit. Two variants, the Mark IA and Mark IB made up the total of 1,566 produced. The Mark I was the mainstay of the Spitfire force during the Battle of Britain, although some Mark IIs were also in service. Even so, the Hawker Hurricane was in service in much greater numbers.

Speed Spitfire. A world speed record attempt was to be made with two modified versions of the Mark I. K9834 was fitted with a special version of the Merlin, short-span wings, and a streamlined cockpit canopy. The attempt was abandoned when the Germans put the record out of reach, so the aircraft was fitted with a standard Merlin XII and used as a high-speed reconnaissance aircraft.

Type 329–Mark II. Fitted with the Merlin XII delivering 1,175hp that gave a top speed increase of some 10mph. Mark IIA and IIB versions were produced in great numbers at Castle Bromwich, as the Supermarine factory at Southampton had been badly damaged by enemy bombing. In all, 750 Mark IIA and 170 Mark IIB Spitfires were built.

Type 348–Mark III. Experimental version powered by a 1,280hp Merlin XX with two-speed supercharger, constant-speed propeller, modified windscreen, retractable tailwheel, and clipped wings. Only one was built, and mainly used as a test airframe for the Merlin 61 engine.

Note. Early reconnaissance versions of the Spitfire were originally designated with a letter suffix, A to F, but this was changed in 1941 to the Roman numeral style, when they became PR Marks I to VI. A great many were converted from Mark IA fighter aircraft and were stripped of all armament, and fitted with a variety of aerial cameras. Extended range fuel and oil tanks were added. Later versions of the PRs were numbered similarly to the fighter designations.

Type 353–Mark IV. This was a single prototype for the later, Griffon-powered, Spitfires. After further modification, it became the Mark XX.

Type 349–Mark V. Powered by several versions of the Merlin engine, and three different wing types, this mark was produced in greater numbers than any other previous Spitfire. Some had clipped wings and more powerful

▲ Pilots helping to push a Spitfire Mark IXB.

▶ Spitfire in flight, 1946.

extended, rather pointed wing tips. Developed to combat the threat of high altitude, enemy reconnaissance aircraft and bombers, this mark was fitted with a partly-pressurised cockpit and had a service ceiling of 41,000ft. The "B" type wing housed its armament of two cannon and four machine guns. Production was 100 aircraft.

Type 351–Mark VII. Powered by the Merlin 60-series engines that introduced the two-speed, two-stage supercharger, this version differed visually in that it had symmetrical radiators under each wing, rather than the asymmetric radiator and oil cooler arrangement of earlier marks, and an enlarged rudder with a pointed tip. Production totalled 140.

Type 360–Mark VIII. In essence, an unpressurised Mark VII, with a Merlin 61 or 63 (1,565 or 1,710hp) and a four-bladed propeller. Carburettor modifications permitted negative g manoeuvring, thus improving previous shortcomings in aerial combat. Many of the 1,652 built were modified for tropical use, and one was later adapted to become what would have been the

engines fitted, for improved low-level performance, drop tanks could be fitted for increased range, and many Mark Vs could carry 250 or 500lb bombs. This mark served with particular distinction in Europe; it was similarly successful in the North Africa campaign and elsewhere, although its specially-adapted, and rather prominent, engine intake dust filter housing somewhat spoiled the classic Spitfire outline on the out-of-Europe version. Including the PR Mark V, production totalled 6,693.

Type 350–Mark VI. This high-altitude variant had a 1,415hp Merlin 47, driving a four-bladed propeller, and

first two-seat Spitfire, but this option was not pursued during the war.

Type 361–Mark IX. Developed around a strengthened Mark V airframe, this version had a Merlin 60-series engine and four-bladed propeller, and several differing wing and armament arrangements. It started out as a short term fix, to counter the threat of the Focke-Wulf 190, and eventually became a major success, with a total of 5,665 built. In its two main variations, one for low altitude with clipped wings, and the other with extended wing tips for high altitude, in addition to the standard fighter version, the Mark IX formed the backbone of the RAF air campaign over Europe.

Type 362–Mark PRX. Based on a converted Mark VII airframe, only 16 were produced, some without the pressurised cockpit. Optimised for high-altitude photo reconnaissance, this unarmed version had a retractable tailwheel, Merlin 64 or 71-series engine, leading edge fuel tanks, and a larger oil tank for increased range. Various camera installations were used.

Type 365–Mark PRXI. Similar to the PRX, but without pressurisation. Fitted with tropical equipment as standard, 461 were built. This out-of-sequence variant actually appeared before the PRX.

Type 366–Mark XII. A significant change with the introduction of the Griffon II or IV, giving some 1,720hp. Another radical difference was that the four-bladed propeller of the Griffon rotated in the opposite direction to Merlin-powered aircraft. Most were clipped-wing variants, and had a retractable tailwheel. 100 were built. Very fast, it was credited with destroying several V1 flying bombs.

Mark PRXIII. Similar to the Mark V, as it used the same camera system, but with the Merlin 32 engine that had been optimised for low-level flight. Fitted with only four machine guns, this mark played a significant part in the Normandy campaign.

Type 373–Mark XIV. Based on the Mark VIII, 957 were built, powered by the Griffon 65 that, by now, developed in excess of 2,000hp. A five-bladed propeller, and a larger fin and rudder, were obvious differences. Later a cut-down rear fuselage, to allow for the new,

◀ Supermarine Spitfire Mark PRXI.

LITTLE BOOK OF THE SPITFIRE

improved-visibility tear-drop canopy was introduced. With two differing wing and armament types, this mark was often used against ground targets when fitted with a 250 or 500lb bomb under the fuselage. It was also fast enough to intercept the infamous V1 flying bomb, on many occasions.

Type 361–Mark XVI. Built alongside the Mark IX, 1,054 were produced with the American-built Packard Merlin 266 driving a four-bladed propeller. Two wing types were fitted, some having wing tip extensions, later batches had clipped wings and a cut-down rear fuselage with the tear-drop canopy.

Type 394–Mark XVIII (Otherwise Mark 18). Redesigned Mark VIII airframe to take the Griffon 63 (2,035hp) or 65 (2,375hp) engine. All 300 built had the tear-drop canopy and an increased fuel capacity.

Type 390–Mark PRXIX (Also known as PR19). Unarmed version based on fuselage of the Mark XIV with a pressurised cockpit, except for the first 22 of the 225 built. Its top speed of 445mph and a service ceiling of 42,600ft made it almost immune from enemy attack. The PRXIX entered

RAF service in May 1944 and made the last operational RAF sortie on 1 April 1954. It remained in service on meteorological work at RAF Woodvale until June 1957.

Type 356–Mark 21. First version to be designated from the outset with Arabic numerals, this mark, although similar in appearance to earlier Spitfires, was a major redesign. Its long nose was typical of the Griffon-powered versions, but its Type C armament wing, with four 20mm cannon, was effectively a complete redesign, with a differently shaped outer wing that was no longer elliptical in plan form. It had an increased span with longer ailerons, and was, structurally, much stiffer. 122 were built.

Type 356–Mark 22. In effect, a Mark 21 with a cut-down rear fuselage and tear-drop canopy. With C or E wing variations, 278 were produced.

Type 356–Mark 24. Similar to the Mark 22, the 54 aircraft built were fitted with the short-barrelled Hispano cannon. Some were also fitted with rocket-rails on their "C" pattern wings. This version featured the Griffon 64 engine that was, by now, giving an output of 2,340hp.

◀ The elliptical planform of a Mark V.

Type 393-Spiteful. A radical development that combined a Spitfire fuselage, a Griffon engine, and a newly-designed laminar flow wing that was believed to give a better high-speed performance. Two early development prototypes were converted from Spitfire Mark XIVs, and kept the original Spitfire tail assembly. The first production prototype had the new wing that also housed a radically redesigned, inwards-retracting undercarriage, and a new tail assembly with an increased area to the fin, rudder and tailplane. There were a number of problems with this new aircraft and, with the advent of jet aircraft, and the imminent ending of hostilities, the Spiteful project was cancelled.

Type 509-Trainer (Tr) Mark IX. After hostilities ceased, Vickers-Armstrong bought back a small number of Mark IX Spitfires, in order to satisfy a strong overseas demand for the aircraft. It was deemed necessary to produce a two-seat trainer version to meet pilot training requirements, although this luxury had not been afforded to the wartime RAF pilots! A total of 26 two-seat Spitfires were produced, wherein the front cockpit was moved forwards, and a second cockpit with a raised seat, domed canopy, and dual-controls, added behind it. Supermarine produced the first official Spitfire two-seater as a private venture, using a Mark VIII as the basis for conversion. In the Middle East, a locally-modified Mark V was flown by No 261 Squadron in 1946; this aircraft could carry a passenger but its rear cockpit was bereft of any flying controls. During the war, the Soviet Union had also produced some two-seat conversions but these were not officially classed as Tr Mark IXs.

The Power and the Growler

▶ The Curtiss
D-12 that had a
direct influence in
the development
of the Kestrel
engine.

The Spitfire, in its many variations, was powered by two main types of engine, first the Merlin and later, the Griffon, both designed by the Rolls-Royce company. Their names followed the customary practice whereby all of the company's piston aero-engines were given the names of birds of prey. Although having a similar appearance, both being liquid-cooled 12-cylinder engines arranged in "V" configuration with six cylinders in each bank, there were considerable differences between the two. Both engines drew heavily on the Rolls-Royce company's experience of high-powered engine design gained from their participation in the Schneider Trophy race: success in this event had ensured the company's continued long association with aero-engines that had begun in WW1, during which conflict they had produced some 60 percent of all British aircraft engines.

In the 1920s, the Fairey Aviation Company, together with the Air Ministry, were not particularly enamoured with the American engine, the Curtiss D-12, which was installed in the Fairey Fox light bomber. The D-12 had been used in the victorious American aircraft, the Curtiss CR-3, in the 1923 Schneider Trophy races and, subsequently, in the Curtiss R3C-2 for the 1925 event. It was a liquid-cooled, in-line V12, and had a capacity of 18.7 litres. Given its racing pedigree, the main reason for the lack of enthusiasm for the D-12 was that it only produced a

relatively meagre 375hp, although this was later increased to 435hp. Due to its configuration as a direct-drive engine, where the propeller rotated at the same speed as the engine crankshaft, and the engine's relatively small internal capacity, there were obvious limitations to its development, as it had relied heavily on the highly specialised aerodynamics of the propeller for its success as a racing engine.

The Curtiss engine was sent to Rolls-Royce for evaluation and, as a result, the British company began to develop the Kestrel engine that was to supersede the D-12 in the Fairey Fox, and help to re-establish the British company in the forefront of aviation engine manufacturing. The requirement for a much higher power rating than the Kestrel's eventual output of around 745hp, for the Schneider Trophy aircraft, led to the development of the famous R-type ("R" signifying Racing), that used a custom-made high-performance fuel, coupled with supercharging. A supercharged engine has its fuel/air mixture compressed, thereby forcing a denser mixture into the cylinders; this has the effect of greatly increasing the engine's volumetric efficiency with the

◀ The R-type Schneider Trophy engine at the Rolls-Royce works in Derby.

dual advantages of both significantly increasing the power output at lower altitudes and, importantly, improving or maintaining power output at higher altitudes, where that of a normally aspirated engine falls off markedly with an increase in altitude.

In its later stages of development, for the 1931 Supermarine S6B, the R-type produced a remarkable output of 2,783hp, although this was due largely to the use of expensive and highly specialised, methanol-based fuels; the engine also had a comparatively short operating life. These factors alone precluded the use of the R-type as a production engine, so the company embarked on a project to design a new high-performance engine that used a conventional 100-octane aviation fuel, would be reliable, and also have an acceptable operational lifespan. The result of their labours was destined to become, probably, the world's most famous piston aero-engine, the Rolls-Royce Merlin.

To fill the void between its 700hp Peregrine and 1,700hp Vulture engines, Rolls-Royce opted for a new engine design, aimed to fill a power output requirement of around 1,100hp, and

be suitable for installation in a single-engined fighter. The new engine was given the designation PV-12 (Private Venture 12 cylinders), as no government funding was involved at this stage. It was originally envisaged that the cooling system would utilise the steam condensing principle but this was later rejected, due to its inherent unreliability and operational performance drawbacks. The company also used sodium-cooled exhaust valves that did much to reduce pre-ignition, thus enhancing the engine's performance and reliability.

The design of the PV-12 retained the cast block principle of the Kestrel engine, in which the cylinders were machined from a large block casting, rather than as individual items. Supercharging was a fundamental part of the design, as was the use of an unpressurised liquid cooling system that was filled with the newly available, and much more efficient, ethylene glycol. In later versions, cooling was achieved by a pressurised 70/30 percent water/ethylene glycol mixture that, apart from being more economical, afforded a lower boiling point at altitude; it also presented a much lower fire hazard in combat. With the eventual placement of a government contract, the newly-named Merlin went into production, but not before Rolls-Royce had incorporated many modifications, and built some 33 prototypes, culminating in the Merlin F that went into production with a rated power output of 1,035hp.

Early versions of the Merlin were first fitted in the Fairey Battle light bomber, and in the Hurricane fighter, although there were many problems with reliability. A far-reaching improvement programme involved the random selection of an engine from the production line, then running it on the test bed, at full power, until it failed. Examination of the failed engine usually revealed the cause of the failure, resulting in redesign or strengthening of the offending component. The inclined valve arrangement, known as the "ramp-head" caused particular problems, and was replaced by the Kestrel-standard,

◀ A Rolls-Royce Kestrel engine.

▶ A Packard-built Merlin as used in the P-51 Mustang.

flat-head arrangement. As a direct result of this improvement programme, the Merlin became one of the most reliable of all aero-engines.

Following on from the letter-designations of the prototypes, A to G, a numerical system was introduced for production versions. The F-engine later became the Merlin I; the G-engine became the Merlin II, and appeared in 1938: it was followed by the Merlin III that drove the new constant-speed propeller. Together, these two versions were produced in large numbers, a total of over 9,700 being fitted in numerous RAF aircraft of the wartime period, from the Spitfire, Hurricane, Battle, and Boulton Paul Defiant I, to the Hawker Henley. With a single-speed, single-stage supercharger, the Merlin III had a capacity of 27 litres, a power output of 1,030hp at 3,000rpm, at an altitude of 5,500ft, and weighed 1,375lb.

Such was the importance of the Merlin to Britain's war effort that a set of plans was sent to America, for safe-keeping, to prevent their falling into enemy hands in the event of an invasion. In due course, the engine was built in large numbers, under licence, in the USA where it was known as the Packard Merlin, after the automotive company that was chosen because of its experience in mass-production engineering. Some parts were redesigned to meet American production standards and tooling methods, as well as allowing it to be assembled by a relatively unskilled workforce. One feature missing from the Packard-built Merlins was the inscription "Rolls-Royce" that appeared on each of the two camshaft covers on the British-built versions.

The Packard Merlin was used to great effect in the American P-51 Mustang fighter, that was also used by the RAF: in its V-1650-3 variant with a two-speed, two-stage supercharger, as installed in the P-51B & C models and the RAF's Mustang III, it produced 1,520hp. Its supercharger, as with all of the two-speed units, had an automatic speed changeover switch that increased the engine boost at a given altitude; there was also a manual override, limited to five minutes use, that could be initiated by the pilot in an emergency combat situation after first breaking a tell-tale wire fitted to the switch.

The success of the Spitfire, and the Hurricane, in the early years of the war

was largely due to the performance and reliability of the Merlin, which went on to famously power the Lancaster and Mosquito in their particular spheres of operations. The Merlin had been developed to such an extent that, in its later versions, it was producing around twice the power output of the Spitfire Mark I's Merlin III (1,030hp);

the two-speed, two-stage supercharged Merlin 130 had a low-altitude output of 2,030hp, and delivered around 1,000hp at altitudes up to 36,000ft. In 1944, a Merlin was reputed to have produced an almost unbelievable 2,640hp, for 15 minutes, on the test bed. Power indeed!

Quite early in the Merlin project, it was believed that there would be a

Merlin, particularly the introduction of the two-stage, two-speed supercharger. Traditionally, the recognised method of increasing the power output of an engine was to increase its swept volume. Although its greater size would also lead to an increase in weight, the potential for increased power output was a key factor in the choice of a larger engine. Enter, the Griffon.

The prototype Griffon was built in 1934. Born out of the engine that had brought success in the Schneider Trophy it was, to all intents and purposes, a de-rated Rolls-Royce R-type. This was a liquid-cooled, in-line V12 engine with a swept volume of some 37 litres capacity. With its ancestor having been developed for high-speed flight, the engine was relatively small in frontal area, considering its large internal capacity; this was a major factor in its favour, as the design criteria for the Griffon dictated that its overall dimensions be close to those of the Merlin, for reasons of interchangeability.

A major departure from the Merlin, and imposed as an Air Ministry design directive for all new aero-engines, rotation of the Griffon was in the opposite direction. This had a similar

◄ A Spitfire in the marking of 340 Squadron, (Free French).

limit to its development, based on the somewhat erroneous premise that its engine capacity of 27 litres would be incapable of producing a significant increase in power, beyond that of its original design calculation. At that time, advances in supercharging design had not reached the levels that were incorporated in later versions of the

▶ A Griffon 58 engine generally used in Shackletons.

opposite effect on the combined torque-reaction and aerodynamic forces that caused an aircraft to veer towards one side of the runway during take-off; the tendency for the aircraft to swing now took place in the opposite direction, often catching out those pilots who were more used to Merlin-engined Spitfires. The Merlin-powered Spitfire tended to swing to the left during the take-off run, whereas Griffon-engined examples swung to the right. Early examples of the Griffon were somewhat less refined compared to its sibling and, reportedly, less smooth than the Merlin. Its larger engine capacity, and a different cylinder firing-order than that of the Merlin, endowed the Griffon with a much deeper and harsher-sounding exhaust note that soon earned it the epithet, "The Growler".

Griffon development was less spectacular than that of the Merlin in respect of the gain in overall power output achieved over that of the first production examples. In the summer of 1940, the Griffon II was rated at

1,720hp at sea level, and 1,495hp at 14,500ft. The Griffon VI that was fitted in the Spitfire Mark XII produced 1,815hp. However, it still produced a substantial increase in rated power, especially with the advent, in 1943, of the Griffon 60-series, fitted with

variants used in the Fairey Firefly, where the power at 9,250ft had risen to 2,245hp. Another major change was made in the Griffon 83 to 88 versions, which incorporated reduction gear units that drove contra-rotating propellers. The Griffon 101 featured a three-speed supercharger unit and was installed in a Spiteful aircraft that reached a speed of 494mph; this combination of engine and airframe suffered many problems during its testing programme and, therefore, did not go into production.

The cessation of hostilities did not bring an end to the Griffon as an operational engine: in addition to it remaining in service, well into the fifties in the later marks of the Spitfire, notably the PRXIX, the Griffon was selected to power the Avro Shackleton four-engined maritime reconnaissance aircraft. Its Griffon 57 and 57A engines were each fitted with dual three-bladed contra-rotating propellers and delivered 2,455hp at low-level. A water/methanol injection system was used to augment engine performance during take-off, particularly in hot climates and when heavily laden. The Griffon remained in front-line service until the retirement of the Shackleton in 1991.

two-speed, two-stage supercharging. The Griffon 65 produced 2,035hp at 7,000ft; the similar Griffon 66 drove a blower for cabin pressurisation in the Spitfire PRXIX.

Further advances in engine output were made in the Griffon 72 and 74

From the Cockpit

► The cockpit of
a Spitfire Mark IX.

"Once you've flown a Spitfire, it spoils you for all other fighters. Every other aircraft seems imperfect in one way or another." – Lt Colonel William R Dunn, USAAF, ex-no 71 (Eagle) Squadron, Royal Air Force

The Spitfire has been described as being "what every well-dressed fighter pilot wore." Almost universally accepted as being a magnificent fighting machine, it was not always the fastest fighter around, but its handling and overall reliability endeared it to those who flew it. Part of its success was due to the fact that every production Spitfire was thoroughly flight tested before being ferried to its operational unit. In 1938, the Vickers-Supermarine company's chief test pilot, Jeffrey Quill, devised the standardised test procedures that, with variations for different marks and engines, were used in testing all development and production Spitfires. Quill headed a team of around 10 or 12 pilots who jointly tested all of the Spitfires built at the Southampton factory. At the Castle Bromwich facility near Birmingham, from 1940 onwards, a team of some 25 pilots carried out the testing of all Spitfires produced at that site. Their chief test pilot, Alex Henshaw, personally carried out the production test flight on a total of some 2,360 Spitfires and Seafires between 1940 and 1946.

The production test flight was not a particularly lengthy process although, from Alex Henshaw's writings, it was a thorough test of the new aircraft's handling and performance. After some initial circuit work of around 10 minutes duration, where the general handling of

The cockpit of a Spitfire Mark IX showing the undercarriage (Chassis) lever on the right.

the aircraft was carried out, in particular that of the trim system which could be adjusted to enable the aircraft to be flown "hands-off", the remainder of the test flight lasted around 20 to 30 minutes. This involved checking the aircraft's climb performance and the rated power output of the engine, calibrated against barometric pressure and temperature graphs. This was followed by a full-power dive in which the trim was set to give "hands and feet-off" stability at speeds of up to 460mph indicated air speed. Henshaw, personally, also performed some aerobatics to determine how good, or bad, that particular aircraft was. It is likely that the other test pilots did similarly, as few pilots would let such an opportunity pass them by!

Henshaw also wrote that earlier marks of Spitfire were much sprightlier handling aircraft than the later more powerful but heavier variants. His testing of the aircraft's roll-rate involved putting the aircraft into a flick-roll to see how many times it rolled; the Mark II and Mark V performed two and a half rolls, the heavier Mark IX gave only one and a half, while later variants failed to reach even that lower figure.

Numerous incidents befell Alex during his long and potentially dangerous test career, including a spate of engine failures related to the skew drive gear in the Merlin engine, of which Henshaw himself suffered 11 out of 14 incidents! Emergency landings were interspersed with the odd crash or two. One of the more serious accidents happened following an engine failure at 800ft, close to Willenhall, near Wolverhampton. In an attempt to avoid a populated area, Henshaw tried to land in a cultivated area and clipped a tree that tore off one wing: the aircraft then hit a house which caused the engine and propeller, and the other wing, to be ripped off. The fuselage finally struck a concrete post and broke in half, leaving the somewhat relieved Alex alive, and able to fly many more Spitfires. On one occasion, on the orders of a higher authority, he carried out a roll manoeuvre while flying above Broad Street, in Birmingham, at a height, according to Henshaw of "around 50 feet."

Getting into the cockpit was no easy task for a Spitfire pilot, especially during the rush of an operational "scramble". After first clambering onto the wing, it was then necessary to step over the sill of the hinged cockpit access door and stand on the pilot's seat cushion, before lowering the body into the sitting position. The word "cushion" is somewhat of a misnomer, as it did little to afford comfort. The seat pan contained the parachute with a dinghy pack on top of it; the latter's pressurised CO_2 inflation cylinder was a prominent feature, being in close contact with the rear end of the unfortunate flyer. Bearing in mind there was no actual cockpit floor, it was better to slide down into position and place the feet directly onto the rudder pedals. The absence of a floor also made things difficult, for pilots and ground crew alike, in the event of an object being dropped into the cockpit. Once installed in the cockpit, the pilot strapped into his parachute harness, connected the lanyard of the dinghy to toggles on his Mae West life-jacket, and tightly secured his seat harness.

Getting out in an emergency situation, given the relatively tight fit, was not an easy process either! In a combat situation with smoke and flames around the cockpit, coupled with g-forces and the possibility of pilot incapacity, it often needed almost

An RAF pilot climbing aboard a Spitfire.

superhuman qualities to escape the confines. Added to all that, the canopy first needed to be jettisoned. In all of its many marks and variations, the Spitfire's canopy offered its own contribution to the difficulty in exiting the pilot's workplace. The recognised procedure for jettisoning the canopy involved the pilot in first lowering his seat to its fullest extent. After undoing his seat harness, he then lowered his head as far as humanly possible, at the same time reaching up to grasp the release knob which, when pulled, acted upon a cable that disengaged the latching pins from the canopy guide rails. Then, using his elbows, the pilot pushed the canopy off the rails. With good fortune, the canopy separated cleanly from the aircraft, allowing the pilot to abandon his aircraft, hopefully, without causing him any further harm. Shorter pilots drew some comfort from their lack of stature should a possible "bail-out" scenario arise.

Throughout the evolution of the Spitfire, there was a steady increase in the many levers and controls that were added around the already limited confines of the cockpit. In addition to the original engine controls, trim wheels, undercarriage and flap levers, there were drop tank and bomb-releases, tailwheel locking (on some later marks) and, for the naval versions, the arrestor hook and wing-folding controls. Pilots wore leather gloves for some protection from the cold, and also to reduce the possibility of laceration or grazing that

could be received from contact with the often sharp edges of the controls themselves, or by their close proximity to other items of cockpit furnishings or aircraft structure. A small crow-bar, clipped to the drop-down cockpit access door, was fitted for use in an emergency situation.

The forward view from the cockpit was obscured while on the ground by the long nose that, due to the tailwheel configuration, pointed upwards from the horizontal. For the pilot to see ahead during taxying, it was necessary for him to weave the aircraft from side to side in a zigzag manner. It was not until the tail lifted during take-off that direct forward vision, over the nose, became possible. The nose also impeded the forward view during the landing phase of flight, leading to the adoption of the Spitfire's classic, curved final-approach to land. Once in the air, the pilot soon discovered the Spitfire's legendary handling qualities. According to Douglas Bader, "this was an aircraft par excellence, with its light, positive and well-harmonised controls." Its wide speed range, from a maximum of 367mph to a landing speed of around 60 to 65mph, was almost without equal.

◀ A squadron of Spitfires taking off.

Due to the less than ergonomic layout of the cockpit, when compared to that of a more modern aircraft, the pilot's movements in the take-off phase of flight, resembled those of an organist, as he moved both feet on the rudder pedals to keep the aircraft straight while, at the same time, changing hands on the grip of the control column in order to perform some of his cockpit duties. Even from a ground observer's standpoint, it was fairly easy to tell the experience, on type, of a Spitfire pilot by the way the aircraft behaved on take-off.

When flown by a relative novice, it would sometimes lurch in a seemingly uncontrolled manner just after becoming airborne, as the pilot transferred his grasp of the spade-handled control column from his right hand to his left, in order to raise the undercarriage. This "change hands" procedure was brought about by the less than ideal placement of some of the key controls. The engine throttle, mixture, and propeller controls were on the left cockpit wall, and the undercarriage lever on the right. Further embarrassment could follow if the pilot had not applied sufficient friction adjustment to the throttle; a combination of engine

◄ A pilot at the controls of a Spitfire.

vibration, and a bumpy airfield, could result in the throttle moving away from the take-off setting and thus reducing power during the critical period, albeit a short one, while he was raising the undercarriage.

During the take-off run, the aircraft was initially kept straight by small rudder adjustments that provided differential braking as the hand-operated brake lever, located on the spade-grip of the control column, was gently squeezed; as the air speed increased, the rudder became effective for maintaining directional control. Shortly after take-off, and on completion of the undercarriage-raising "organ recital", the pilot's hands then resumed their original tasks, after first giving a short squeeze of the brake lever to stop wheel rotation before the undercarriage entered its close-fitting housing. Once safely airborne, the engine throttle next required an intentional reduction in power to the 'climb' boost-setting, and the aircraft's trim controls that were also located on the left side of the cockpit, likewise needed some adjustment.

Merlin-powered Spitfires were considered to be much smoother when compared to their Griffon-engined relatives. Although they rotated in opposite directions, with a consequent opposite effect on torque and gyroscopic forces, both versions had one thing in common – power in abundance! An American pilot, Jeff Ethell, sadly no longer with us, described the feeling of flying a Griffon-powered Spitfire as being "… similar to that of driving a hot rod car, the feeling of unbridled horsepower being transmitted to the pilot through the seat of his pants." On later marks, the overall throttle lever movement was around four inches, effectively giving over 400hp for each inch of movement. Although Douglas Bader had described the controls of early marks of Spitfire as being well-harmonised, later versions were reportedly much less so: the elevator controls remained light and required a delicate touch in order that smooth changes in the pitch axis could be made; the rudder was relatively stiff in deflection, particularly at higher speeds, as were the ailerons, which needed a strong hand.

When landing, the Spitfire was characterised by its curved final approach path to the runway, necessary because of the limited forward view

▲ A Spitfire
Mark II about to
touch down.

from the cockpit. In most other respects, landing was not overly dramatic, bearing in mind its narrow-tracked undercarriage. With docile handling down to a very slow speed its sometimes inexperienced pilot was usually able to make a decent three-point touchdown. Inevitably, there were occasional mishaps during the return to terra firma, some resulting from undercarriage malfunction or battle damage, or as a result of over-enthusiastic use of the brakes during the landing run, which caused the aircraft to nose-over.

The handling characteristics, especially those of some later variants

▲ A Spitfire of No 72 Squadron on patrol.

would, at first, appear to be contrary to the requirements for aerial combat. However, coupled with the aerodynamics bestowed on it by Mitchell's design team, the intensive flight testing programme of the airframe

and engine, and the skill and courage of those who flew it, the Spitfire achieved its deserved, legendary status as a fighting machine. Its capability of performing, and maintaining, a very tight turning radius often gained its pilot the upper hand over an adversary. The Mark I, with its eight Browning 0.303in machine guns or, four machine guns and two 20mm cannon, was the version of the Spitfire that, together with the Hurricane, formed the mainstay of RAF Fighter Command at the outbreak of WW2.

At the commencement of hostilities in 1939, orders had been placed for a total of 2,143 Spitfires. The first RAF unit, No 19 Squadron at Duxford, had received its first 1,030hp Merlin II-engined, Mark I aircraft between August and December 1938 and, by the following September, a further nine squadrons were similarly equipped. Deliveries of the Mark II, with the more powerful Merlin XII of 1,175hp, began in June 1940, although it did not appear in large numbers until much later in that year. By the early part of July 1940, 19 squadrons of Spitfires were operational. It was mainly the Mark I, together with the more numerous Hurricane, that carried out the task of defending Britain from the air in those critical days of war.

Like a Duck to Water

Supermarine Spitfire float-planes. When the Germans invaded Norway in April 1940, there arose an urgent requirement for a float-plane fighter aircraft that could operate from the Norwegian Fjords in the, as yet, unoccupied parts of that territory. Due to the difficult terrain of the region, and the lack of airfields or other ground that would be suitable for aircraft operations outside of the enemy-occupied areas, the only option was for a water-based fighter.

The task was given to the Vickers-Supermarine company who had a wealth of experience in high-speed, water-borne flight; their Schneider Trophy-winning experience could be vital to the successful and prompt completion of a suitable aircraft. Its ancestry made the Spitfire a prime candidate for conversion to a float-plane configuration. A Mark I Spitfire was selected for modifications at the Woolston factory. Due to the urgency of the military situation in Norway, there was insufficient time to design, build, and test a set of floats for the Spitfire from first principles; therefore, a set of floats from the Fleet Air Arm fighter, the Blackburn Roc, were used as a starting point for the conversion.

Tests, using a one-seventh scale model, were carried out in the hydrodynamics test tank facility at Farnborough, where the Supermarine company had tested their S6-series of aircraft. The results were promising, although the vertical tail surfaces needed to be increased to counter the effects of the large side areas of the two floats. Accordingly, a ventral fin was added, in place of the now redundant tailwheel. However, the military situation in

Norway soon deteriorated, ending in withdrawal by the Allies, so the float-plane Spitfire project, informally known as the Narvik Nightmare, was cancelled. With the ventral fin and floats removed, and its tailwheel assembly refitted, the aircraft was converted back to its original fighter role.

Early 1942 saw the revival of the float-plane fighter project, this time for use in the eastern Mediterranean and Aegean, following the German invasion of the Greek islands. The objective was to disrupt the supply chain to the occupying forces that relied heavily on air transport; a float-plane fighter was seen as one possible option, operating from sheltered waters in that region, and relying on the British bases in Egypt

for its own support needs. Resulting from the promise shown in the earlier float-plane project, the Spitfire was again selected for conversion, this time a Mark V. Powered by a Merlin 45 driving a four-bladed propeller, this aircraft was fitted with two floats, a ventral fin extension in place of the tailwheel, and a Vokes-type air filter was added to the carburettor intake under the engine. Additionally, four strong lifting-points were fitted, two forward of the cockpit, and the other two behind, for hoisting the complete aircraft from the water during transfer to a ship or shore facility. For flight testing, the aircraft was fitted with a spin-recovery parachute, the location of which required the installation of a protective guard in front

of the rudder horn balance to prevent the parachute line from fouling the rudder. Fortunately, the spin-recovery system was not called upon.

The Mark V float-plane made its first flight on 12 October 1942, flown by Jeffrey Quill. Aside from the change from the Vokes to an Aero-Vee filter, and an extension forwards of the engine intake duct to prevent the ingestion of spray, there were few modifications made. Armed to the Mark VB standard, this aircraft, and a further two that had been converted by the Folland Aircraft Company, arrived by sea in Egypt in October 1943. By the time of their arrival, the original requirement for float-plane fighters had been overtaken by events, particularly the loss of the islands of Kos and Leros to enemy forces: the aircraft were instead sent to operate from the Great Bitter Lake on the Suez Canal. Despite the encumbrance of their float gear, the Spitfire VB float-planes were still quite reasonable performers, with a top speed of 324mph at 19,500ft, a service ceiling of 33,000ft, and a maximum climb rate of 2,450ft/min at 15,500ft.

The war in the Pacific theatre was also seen as an area of operations in

which a float-plane fighter could serve a useful purpose, especially around the many islands. This time, a Spitfire Mark IX was the basis for conversion which, on completion, gave it a broadly similar external appearance to its water-borne Mark V predecessors. Again, the project did not reach fruition as the float-plane fighter concept was abandoned, the only Mark IX that had been fitted with floats being converted back to a land-based fighter. Its test pilot, Jeffrey Quill, wrote in his appraisal of its qualities: "The Spitfire IX on floats was faster than the standard Hurricane. Its handling on the water was extremely good and its only unusual feature was a tendency to 'tramp' from side to side on the floats, or to 'waddle' a bit when at high speed in the plane" – the reference to "the plane" being the point at which its speed over the water caused the aircraft to rise onto the stepped portion of the floats.

At the outbreak of war in 1939, carrier-based Fleet defence was the province of such ageing aircraft designs as the Gloster Sea Gladiator; this was shortly to be supplemented in 1940 by the Fairey Fulmar, a development of the land-based Fairey Battle light bomber. At the time, it was Royal

was later removed, opening the way for the introduction of single-seat fighter aircraft into the Fleet Air Arm.

Some American lend-lease carrier aircraft were drafted into service, to help fill the shortfall, namely the Grumman Martlet, as was the introduction of the British-built Hawker Sea Hurricane, a conversion of the ageing land-based fighter. The adaptability and inherent

Navy policy that all of its carrier-borne aircraft should carry a navigator: this had imposed a design requirement for a minimum of two crew-members to be carried that resulted in the Fulmar being too heavy. Its weight reduced its climb performance and, therefore, imposed a consequent reduction in its ability to engage with enemy fighters. The Fairey Firefly was powered by a 1,730hp Griffon, instead of the Merlin of the Fulmar, and with the greater fire-power of four 20mm cannon over the Fulmar's eight machine guns, was not destined to reach carrier squadrons until late in 1943. The two-crew stipulation

◄◄◄ Spitfires banking in shafts of sunlight.

◄◄ A Super-marine Seafire flying over an Invincible-Class aircraft carrier in 1943.

◄ The Spitfire VB float-plane W3760 on the point of take-off.

▼ A British Spitfire takes off from USS Wasp.

► Seafires
onboard an
aircraft carrier.

reliability of the Spitfire, in addition to its excellent performance and air combat qualities, was soon to see it take on a different role than that for which it was originally intended. Few could ever have envisaged, during its design and early development, that there was even the slightest possibility of this aircraft being utilised in a maritime role.

Supermarine Seafire (officially named Sea Spitfire). This was a naval version of the Spitfire and became the first modern, carrier-based fighter to join the inventory of the Royal Navy. Principally intended for use on aircraft carriers, the Seafire was endowed with equipment necessary for operations on that type of vessel, including a tail hook, strong-points for catapult attachment, and on later variants, wing-folding arrangements. In its earliest form, the Seafire was less than ideal for carrier-borne operations, particularly because of its narrow-track undercarriage, but some of the disadvantages were outweighed by its performance as a fast, rapid-climbing fleet defence fighter.

Type 340–Seafire Mark IB. Even before the outbreak of war, the Admiralty had, in 1938, made an approach to the Air Ministry for a

▼ A restored
Supermarine
Mark IX Spitfire.

naval version of the Spitfire but their approaches were turned down, as were a further two requests in early 1940. The following year, the Royal Navy (RN) was offered some modified Spitfire Mark I land-planes to fill their urgent combat fighter needs, although their Lordships at the Admiralty had demanded they be given the latest Mark V version. Their wishes were fulfilled when, in September 1941, the Admiralty was allowed to place an order for 250 Spitfire Mark VA and VB aircraft, even though they had not yet finalised the list of modifications that were necessary for carrier operations. To assist in training of the RN pilots, the RAF loaned a large number of Mark VA and VBs, the

◄ Landing personnel running to disengage a landing hook.

majority having first been fitted with tail hooks.

In service, the main drawback in operating the Seafire I was its relative fragility, as it had been designed without the much greater stresses imposed by carrier operations being taken into account. The limited forward visibility from the cockpit during the approach to the flight deck made life especially difficult for the pilot, as the carrier was often moving vertically, as well as forwards, during this critical phase of flight. In the subsequent landing, often a very heavy one when compared with a typical airfield arrival, an undercarriage collapse was commonplace, as was damage caused to the rear fuselage structure by the rebound of the tail hook from the deck, following a failed

attempt to trap the arrestor wire. It has been claimed that more Seafire I aircraft were lost in landing accidents than those

due to enemy action.

Type 357–Seafire Mark IIC. The specifically-modified "naval" version of

the Mark V was known as the Seafire II. This mark featured a substantial strengthening of the airframe in critical areas, provision of hard points for the carriage of under-wing stores, and a major redesign of the main undercarriage; this was lengthened, and raked forward, to improve both its landing characteristics, and its general deck handling capabilities. Unfortunately, little could be done about improving the forward view. Notwithstanding its drawbacks, the Seafire was a welcome addition to the carrier force, bringing its known outstanding capabilities as an interceptor fighter to its new role as a fleet defender. Somewhat heavier than the land-based aircraft it was based on, it was a great improvement over the previous fleet defence aircraft such as the Sea Gladiator, although the by now ageing Sea Hurricane fighter did sterling work in similar circumstances. As for the Seafire, the Sea Hurricane had been converted from a land-based fighter.

Type 358–Seafire Mark III. In 1943, the Seafire Mark III entered service and was the first Seafire to have a manually-operated foldable wing for below-deck storage. After the first batch of Mark IIIs, later LF Mark IIIs that were optimised for low-level operations, and fitted with the Merlin 55M engine, formed the bulk of over 1,000 produced. Some of the earlier Mark II and III fighters were each fitted with two F24 cameras and used in the maritime fighter reconnaissance role, in which they proved highly successful.

Type 337–Seafire Mark XV. This version's out-of-sequence numbering resulted from an attempt at rationalising the numbering across the various marks of Spitfire and Seafire. The Mark XV was the sea-going equivalent of the Spitfire XII with two symmetrical under-wing radiators, a 1,750hp Griffon VI driving a four-bladed propeller and broader-chord rudder. One obvious difference was the retractable tailwheel and arrestor hook.

◄ A beautifully restored example of a Seafire XVII.

Type 395–Seafire Mark XVII.
The last batch of Mark XVs built were
modified to become the Mark XVII,
and had a cut-down rear fuselage, a
curved windscreen, bubble canopy,
and wing fuel tanks. It also featured a
strengthened undercarriage, and a larger
area fin and rudder. As the Spitfire
numbering was changed from Roman
to Arabic numerals around this time, so
was that of the Seafire, their marks being
numbered from 40 onwards; the Mark
XVII is also, somewhat confusingly,
known as the Mark 41.

Type 388–Seafire 45. The navalised
equivalent of the Spitfire Mark 21,
with the new wing and Griffon 61
engine. In a short production run, only
50 were built.

Type 388–Seafire 46. First
Seafire to have the dual three-bladed
contra-rotating propeller, that
effectively eliminated the torque
swing on take-off, fitted as standard.
The absence of wing-folding
contributed to the relatively short
production run of only 24 examples.
Originally part of the Admiralty's
Spitfire Mark V order placement, this
order was transferred to an order for
the Spitfire 21 before eventually being

designated as the Seafire 46.

Type 388–Seafire 47. Probably the best of the Seafires, this mark had a 2,200hp Griffon driving a contra-rotating propeller, and the enlarged tailplane and fin/rudder assembly from the Spiteful. A total of 90 were built.

Type 383–Seafang. The navalised version of the Spiteful, the first examples, designated Seafang F31, being based on a conversion from a Spiteful XV. Only nine were built. The Seafang F32 had a larger fuel capacity, and featured folding wing tips,

than respectable 4,630ft/min. Only two reached final assembly from a batch of 10 sets of parts made.

Although it was very fast, the Seafang, having been derived from the Spiteful, the fastest propeller-driven piston-engined aircraft ever built in Britain with a top speed of 494mph, was not particularly good at low speeds. Its performance did not offer much of an improvement over that of the excellent Seafire 47, so the Fleet Air Arm selected the Hawker Sea Fury for the fleet fighter role instead.

The Seafire in its various guises also attracted attention from Commonwealth and foreign naval air services, and was even tested in the USA as a potential choice for the US Navy ship-borne fighter; however, no order was forthcoming. Thirty-five Seafires saw service with the Royal Canadian Navy between 1946 and 1954, operating from the carrier HMCS Warrior and naval shore bases. The RN Fleet Air Arm operated Seafires on front-line duties until 1951, and the type remained in service with the RNVR until late in 1954.

◄ A cannon-armed Seafire on the deck of HMS Indomitable.

a 2,350hp Griffon 89 or 90 driving a new Rotol-designed, dual three-bladed contra-rotating propeller. Armed with four 20mm cannon, it had provision for carrying two 1,000lb bombs or four 60lb rockets. With a service ceiling of 41,000ft, its initial climb rate was a more

Eyes in the Skies

Britain was not fully prepared for the outbreak of the war in 1939, both in its shortage of modern fighters and bombers, and its lack of suitable reconnaissance aircraft. Originally, it was planned to use the Bristol Blenheim bomber in the long-range reconnaissance role, and the Westland Lysander for shorter ranges. At the start of the war, photographic reconnaissance was carried out mostly by operational squadrons on an ad hoc basis. A Blenheim carried out the first operational RAF sortie of the war when a Mark IV of No 139 Squadron flew a photo reconnaissance mission over German naval forces, near the German coast, on the first day of the conflict on 3 September 1939.

Both of these aircraft types were susceptible to attack from the air by enemy fighters; they were also extremely vulnerable to ground or ship-based anti-aircraft fire. During the early part of the war in France and Belgium, the Lysander had proved no match for the enemy due largely to its slow speed, lack of defensive armament, and poor

▶ A Spitfire Mark XI with split pair camera ports under the fuselage, aft of the wing roots.

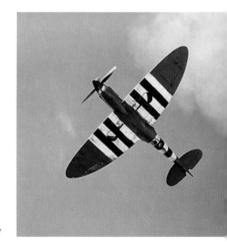

agility. Of the 174 Lysanders sent to France, 88 were lost in the air, and a further 30 were destroyed on the ground. Clearly, Britain needed a much more suitable alternative; this had been recognised, and even suggested, prior to the outbreak of war. The concept of a fast monoplane, optimised for photographic reconnaissance duties; began to be realised in October 1939, when two Mark I Spitfires were selected for conversion.

Shortly before the onset of war, an Australian-born RAF veteran of WW1, Sidney Cotton, had been recruited by the British intelligence services. Cotton, whose business and social activities could be described as less than conventional, had a wealth of flying experience, including high-altitude flight and aerial photography. In the period leading up to the commencement of hostilities, Cotton had carried out a number of covert photographic missions under the guise of business trips that took him near to, and sometimes overhead, German military installations and other strategic industrial locations in his Lockheed Electra Junior. This aircraft had been financed by the British intelligence

◀ Sidney Cotton, who pioneered high altitude photography.

services, and was fitted with three concealed F24 cameras, operated by a hidden control under the pilot's seat: Cotton had actually taken photographs of German installations, undetected, while carrying a senior Luftwaffe officer, Albert Kesselring, on a "joy-ride" over Berlin. The Electra was claimed to have been the last civilian aircraft to leave that city prior to the outbreak of WW2.

With his already vast experience, in both high-altitude aviation and

► Spitfire Mark IIC serial P7350 is the oldest airworthy example in the world and the only Spitfire still flying today to have actually fought in the Battle of Britain.

aerial photography, Cotton was a good choice to head the new RAF No 1 Photographic Development Unit (PDU) at Heston, later to become No 1 Photographic Reconnaissance Unit (PRU) based at Hendon. Initially designated as No 2 Camouflage Unit, the unit's somewhat ironical naming was intended to deflect unwanted attention from its real activities, the new unit began its task of improving the RAF's rather poor reconnaissance capability. This it did to great effect: by the end of the war, RAF reconnaissance had improved beyond all expectations, due mainly to the efforts of No 1 PDU. After perfecting techniques in the more traditional methods of aerial photography of ground targets, from aircraft operating at great altitudes and high speeds, their pioneering use of both oblique and stereoscopic photography was fundamental, later in the war, in countering the threat of the German

V1 and V2 weapons. These new photographic techniques revealed the exact locations of the characteristic V1 launching ramps, and many of the V2 launching and storage sites. Cotton also had his aircraft painted in a light blue

▼ A 1942 Supermarine Spitfire Mark IX.

finish, similar to that of his Electra, a colour that made the, mostly unarmed, reconnaissance aircraft difficult to see while in flight.

At the outset, Cotton's unit operated the Blenheim, which he claimed was too slow, but he successfully lobbied higher authority for his unit to be given the Spitfire. The first two aircraft allocated to the unit were to be the precursors of around 1,000 Spitfires that were either converted, or built specifically, for the Photographic Reconnaissance (PR) role. Although much less in the public domain than their much-lauded fighter cousins, for reasons of military necessity in wartime, their contribution to British and Allied operations was significant; regrettably, the reconnaissance Spitfires, and the men that flew them, did not achieve the widespread recognition their exploits deserved.

There were many developments of the reconnaissance Spitfire; as had happened with the fighter, these aircraft inherited a similarly bewildering method of numbering types and variants. Until late 1941, Spitfire PR types were identified by letters, the six versions produced prior to that time having been allocated the letters A to F. This led to some confusion with the Spitfire wing types which bore similar letter designations. From the autumn of 1941, letters were replaced by Roman numerals, the six types that had been previously identified by letters now becoming PR Marks I to VI, although the first two had largely

◀ Spitfire Mark XI EN 409 which was used in high-speed diving trials in 1944.

been superseded by this time. However, the new identifiers brought still further confusion to the Spitfire story, as the Spitfire Mark VII fighter, and the PR Mark VII, are substantially different aircraft: the fighter Mark VII had a Merlin 60 or 70-series engine and a B-type wing, with two 20mm cannon and four 0.303in machine guns; the PR Mark VII had a Merlin 45 engine, a large oil tank under the nose and, being based on the Spitfire IA, had an eight machine-gun wing, plus an extra fuel tank in the rear fuselage. From the PR Mark X onwards, discrete numbers were

▶ Photograph of the breached Möhne Dam taken from a Spitfire PR IX.

allocated to either the fighter version or the PR version, thereby simplifying things somewhat, although there was a further fly in the Spitfire ointment. The introduction of an occasional Fighter Reconnaissance (FR) version, some of which bore a combination of Roman numerals *and* a letter suffix, e.g. the Spitfire FR Mark XIVe, added to the already chaotic Spitfire mark identification system.

The early PRs were, in essence, fairly straightforward adaptations of the Spitfire Mark IA. Guns were removed to reduce weight, and their ports faired over. Joints between various parts of the aircraft structure, access panel gaps, and the like, were closed over to reduce drag and, therefore, increase speed. With the addition of cameras, this was a reasonable starting point for what was eventually to become a highly-optimised and successful photographic reconnaissance aircraft. Together with the de Havilland Mosquito PR aircraft, it was a valuable asset in both the air and ground offensives against enemy forces, and strategic targets, in mainland Europe, North Africa, and other campaigns east of Suez.

PR Type A (PR Mark I). With

▲ A Spitfire PR XIX with a Griffon engine driving two contra-rotating propellers.

its guns removed and their ports faired over, this mark had an improved-visibility cockpit canopy that featured a large transparent perspex blister on each side. A downward-facing F24 camera was installed in the inner gun bay of each wing. One of this type became the first Spitfire to operate overseas when it joined British Expeditionary Forces (BEF) in France, in November 1939, flying its first mission that was aborted due to cloud cover over Aachen, on 18 November. Both aircraft were later converted to PR Mark III standard.

PR Type B (PR Mark II).
Improvements over the PR Mark I included the addition of an extra 29-gallon fuel tank behind the cockpit, and the F24 camera was upgraded from a 5in to an 8in focal-length lens. The PR Mark II was first used on 10 February 1940, when this aircraft successfully photographed the German naval bases at Emden and Wilhelmshaven.

PR Type C (PR Mark III).
Entered service in March 1940. The first PR to be produced in numbers; a total of 40 were produced by converting existing marks of Spitfire fighters. Extended range was endowed by the 30-gallon capacity fuel tank that was fitted under the port wing; a blister under the starboard wing housed two F24 cameras with 8in lenses. Provision was also made for an additional F24 camera to be vertically-mounted in the rear fuselage.

PR Type D (PR Mark IV).
Nicknamed "the bowser", its 114 gallons of fuel made it capable of reaching Stettin, on the Baltic coast of Germany; at 2,000 miles, its range was the greatest of all early Spitfires. Entering service in October 1940, a total of 229 aircraft were produced. Each PR Mark IV was given a letter code relating to the complement of camera(s) carried: W – two F8 with 20in lenses; X – one F24 with a 14in lens; Y – one F52 with a 36in lens; S – two F24 with 14in lenses.

PR Type E (PR Mark V). Only one of this mark was produced but it blazed the trail for others to be fitted

◀ Spitfire P7350 "Enniskillen".

▶ Spitfire PR XI,
serial PL965 was
built in 1944.

with a similar obliquely-mounted camera; this development gave the Spitfire the ability to carry out low-level photography at 90° to the direction of travel, thus eliminating the need for direct overflight of the target and thus reduced the risk of being hit by enemy defensive fire.

PR Type F (PR Mark VI). This was an interim, out-of-sequence design that was produced prior to the appearance of the PR Mark IV; the first of the 15 built entered service in March 1940. It had two under-wing fuel tanks, each holding 30 gallons, and an additional fuselage tank that together gave the aircraft sufficient endurance for a round trip to Berlin of up to four and a half hours duration. The first Berlin flight was made on 14 March 1941 with two F24 cameras with 8in lenses, later replaced by two F8 cameras with 20in lenses. Some Mark VIs carried an oblique-mounted F24 with a 14in lens.

PR Mark VII. This was the first Spitfire PR variant to be fitted with armament, as the low-level role took it into areas that were patrolled by enemy fighters. Fitted with the eight machine guns from the fighter Mark IA, it also carried the extra-range fuselage tank; cameras were two vertically-mounted F24s, with 5in and 14in lenses respectively and an oblique F24 with a 14in lens. The oblique camera could be fitted so that it faced either port, or starboard. Production was 45 PR Mark VIIs, converted from Mark V fighters.

PR Mark IX. A short-term fix whereby a small number of Mark IX fighters were stripped of their armament and fitted with two vertically-mounted cameras.

FR Mark IX. Used for low-level and medium-level reconnaissance, these were the most heavily-armed of all the reconnaissance Spitfire marks. A true fighter reconnaissance aircraft, they all carried the standard gun arrangement of the Mark IX fighter, together with an oblique F24 camera.

PR Mark X. Another out-of-sequence variant that appeared in early 1944, almost a year after the Mark XI. Based on the Mark VII fighter fuselage, it had the wings of a Mark XI but with two 66-gallon fuel tanks in place of the guns. Withdrawn from service in September 1945, only 16 were produced.

PR Mark XI. Produced in greater numbers than any other PR variant

with a total of over 470 having been built. It was based on a much modified PR Mark IX fuselage that had the extra fuselage fuel tank, as for that fitted on many PRs, and wing fuel tanks. Entering service in the summer of 1943, it was the first PR variant to be fitted with a "universal" camera installation that would allow rapid changes between the selection of cameras it could carry. These ranged from two F52 x 36in focal length, two F8 x 20in, one F52 x 20in and two F24 x 14in, with another F24 x 14in (or 8in) mounted obliquely. Some aircraft carried an additional F24 x 5in camera mounted behind a wheel-well for the low-to-medium altitude ranges of photographic work.

PR Mark XIII. Entering service in late summer of 1942, the Mark XIII was an armed low-level reconnaissance fighter with a four-gun defensive armament. Although its range was somewhat limited by its gun installation, it proved invaluable in the preparations for the Normandy landings in 1944. It was converted from the Mark I and Mark V fighters, and the PR Mark VII. Cameras were three F24s, two vertical and one oblique.

◀ A comparatively rare Spitfire Tr 9 two-seater.

PR Mark XIX.
Built by combining the
fuselage of the Mark
XIV fighter with the
pressurised cabin of the
PR Mark X, this being
incorporated into all,
except for the first 22
examples, of the 225 that
were built. The wings
were those of the PR
Mark X. The Mark XIX
was the only Griffon-
powered PR variant,
and had an internal fuel
capacity of up to 254
gallons. It was cleared to
carry a drop tank with
a further 170 gallons,
although the largest
used on operations held
70 gallons. The camera
installation allowed for
two vertical cameras and
one oblique camera on
the port side: vertical
cameras were usually
F8s with 14in or 20in
focal length lenses or
F52s with 20in lenses,
the oblique camera was

an F24 with either an 8in or 14in lens. The PR Mark XIX was the ultimate PR version: its top speed of 445mph, and a service ceiling of 42,600ft, made it an almost impossible feat for a Luftwaffe fighter to catch it. Its first flight was in April 1944, becoming operational in the following month. Remaining in RAF service as an operational reconnaissance aircraft for one month short of 20 years, its swan-song took place on 1 April 1954. The PR XIX continued to fly for a further three years, three aircraft being used on meteorological duties with the Temperature and Humidity Flight, at RAF Woodvale, until their retirement on 10 June 1957.

◀ A clipped wing Spitfire XIV. Note the five-bladed propeller.

Spitfire Notes and Anecdotes

▶ Spitfire P7350 behind a Hawker Hurricane.

There are around 50 Spitfires, and a small number of Seafires, still flying today. The actual number fluctuates from year to year, due to some of them undergoing heavy maintenance, partial restoration or, in extreme cases, a complete rebuild. The fact that so many are still capable of flight, over 70 years after the prototype K5054 first flew, is tribute to the dedicated and painstaking work of Spitfire enthusiasts the world over. In addition to those aircraft that are capable of flight, there are also a large number on static display in museums and private exhibitions. Such is the demand for a Spitfire to be put on display that many replicas have been produced. Had it not been such a successful and historic aircraft, this aircraft would still be in great demand: its classic lines have an aesthetic appeal that places the Spitfire firmly in the category – "If it looks right, it is right."

The Spitfire is known, and loved, by many who were yet to be born when this charismatic aircraft was both a symbol of hope, and defender of Britain, in the dark days of war. Spitfires can regularly be seen in flight at air shows. The RAF Battle of Britain Memorial Flight (BBMF) is in great demand for fly-pasts at ceremonial events and air displays, and can be seen regularly with one or more of its five airworthy Spitfires. A single Spitfire usually flies in a formation of three aircraft, together with a Hurricane and a Lancaster Bomber, paying tribute to the longevity

▶ The clipped wing Spitfire Mark V showing the external fuel tank that increased the operating range of the aeroplane.

of these amazing aircraft. As the name of the unit signifies, each flight that takes place is an airborne memorial to those who fought, and died, in the defence of their country in the great aerial conflicts of WW2. The appearance of the BBMF formation at an air show or other event is not only a visual delight; it is one of the few occasions that the evocative sound of the Merlin engine, itself a memorable occasion, can be heard in its natural environment by aviation enthusiasts and the general public alike.

Delivered in August 1940, Spitfire Mark IIA serial number P7350 is the oldest airworthy example remaining, and is operated by the BBMF. It served with Nos 266, 603, 616 and 64 Squadrons of the RAF and later, with 57 OTU. In 1946 it was sold for scrap, together with its aircraft log book, to John Dale & Sons: fortunately, they realised the importance of this aircraft, and it was reprieved, later being safely delivered to the RAF Colerne Museum. In 1967 it went into "make-up" in readiness for its starring role in the film *The Battle of Britain*: after filming had been completed, it was allocated to the BBMF where it has remained ever since.

The transition from the outmoded

fighters, such as the Gloster Gladiator that were equipping front-line RAF squadrons at the start of WW2, onto the Spitfire, was not a particularly trouble-free exercise. Until then, fighter pilots had flown slower, open-cockpit aircraft with a fixed undercarriage: many found it difficult to adapt to the more modern newcomer, especially as it was a single-seater, with no trainer variant to ease the path to competence. The original canopy on the Spitfire Mark I had its top and sides flush with the line of the fuselage; the restricted headroom was particularly claustrophobic and made things difficult for taller pilots, many of whom, as a result, flew with the canopy open. The introduction of the bulged, Malcolm-type cockpit canopy gave a large increase in headroom while, at the same time, substantially improving the all-round visibility when airborne. While on the ground, nothing could be done that would greatly improve the pilot's forward visibility. The zigzag manoeuvre that typified the Spitfire while taxying was, in itself, responsible for the occasional, inadvertent "coming together" with another aircraft or item of ground equipment. The net result, for the hapless pilot involved, was to spend a few quaking moments in front of the CO's desk; for the maintenance crew, it was an unscheduled addition to their workload.

The retractable undercarriage of the Spitfire was also unfamiliar to many pilots, and their failing to lower the undercarriage before landing was the cause of many landing accidents: further embarrassment was heaped upon the unfortunate flier when it was discovered that he had previously switched off the undercarriage warning klaxon, due to its often spurious operation caused by vibration or other mechanical action. A narrow-tracked undercarriage made cross-wind landings hazardous for the less-experienced, although the aircraft's good low-speed qualities were relatively forgiving in most other situations. A pronounced swing on take-off was another trap for the unwary, newly-converted Spitfire pilot who was hitherto not familiar with a combination of prodigious amounts of torque and the aerodynamic and gyroscopic forces involved; some more experienced pilots were also caught unawares. Coupled with the unergonomic cockpit layout, any (or all) of the foregoing possibilities conspired to provide the new pilot

with an exciting time. Having gained the necessary experience on type, and mastered the art of flying, and fighting, in the Spitfire, most were totally captivated by it.

Probably one of the most famous Spitfires of the war was that flown by (then) Wing Commander J E (Johnnie) Johnson, a Mark IX, serial number EN398. In 1943, with his current tally of seven confirmed enemy aircraft destroyed and two shared "kills", four probables, and five damaged, Johnson was posted to RAF Kenley to lead a wing of four Canadian units: two squadrons flew the Spitfire Mark V, and two the Mark IX. Johnson had already flown the Mark V but soon chose the Mark IX as his personal aircraft. He quickly fell for his new mount; after a test flight, he described her as "… very fast, the engine was sweet and she responded to the controls as only a thoroughbred can. I decided that she should be mine, and I never had occasion to regret the choice."

He had his initials painted on her as the squadron code "JE-J" and, instead of the usual "spread" pattern of gun harmonisation, had the aircraft's cannon and machine guns re-harmonised to

converge at a single point in front of the aircraft. This was a mark of confidence in his own air gunnery skills as this left little margin for error, although his shots on target would be concentrated to deadly effect. Apart from a small idiosyncrasy of EN398, in that the aircraft that showed a permanent off-centre indication on the turn-and-bank gauge when in straight and level flight, both pilot and machine were as one, and Johnson flew her almost exclusively while in command of the Canadian wing. In six months of flying EN398, Johnson added another 12 "kills" and five others shared, with a further six damaged with one other shared. The aircraft's own tally of 15 and one-sixth enemy aircraft destroyed, and six and a half damaged, is even more remarkable as it never suffered damage from enemy fire, neither did it fail to complete a mission through technical malfunction.

Johnson's experience ranged across three marks of Spitfire: apart from the aforementioned Mark IX, he also flew the Mark VB and the XIVe. His total of 38 enemy aircraft destroyed made him the top scoring British pilot of the war, a total that was all the more creditable in that all of his victories were against fighter aircraft. The fate of his famous mount EN398 was rather ignominious for such a celebrated aircraft of her day; after spending some of the wartime period being repaired after an accident while on charge with a Canadian squadron, followed by a lengthy period in storage, she became a training aircraft for French pilots in late 1954. After several post-war years in storage, EN398 was unceremoniously sold for scrap in October 1949.

There are many stories surrounding the history of the Spitfire, some tell of heroic deeds carried out in air combat, or during offensives against ground targets, while other tales recount events that covered the relatively mundane, day-to-day lives of RAF personnel during the wartime and subsequent operations. Occasionally, there occurred an event that even those involved would describe as being somewhat unusual, or even bizarre. The practice of carrying out the ground running of a newly installed engine, followed by an air test, is a routine that will be familiar to those with knowledge of RAF aircraft engineering procedures. A similar routine, in the form of an engine power check, takes place prior to every take-off. On most occasions, things go relatively smoothly: sometimes, things do not always go exactly according to plan, as was the case in one of these happenings that has become firmly embedded in Spitfire history.

Those present on Hibaldstow Airfield in Lincolnshire, a satellite of RAF Kirton-in-Lindsey, one day in early 1945, witnessed an event that had started out as commonplace, but subsequently unfolded in a remarkable

◀ Group Captain Douglas Bader sits in the cockpit of his Supermarine Spitfire, preparing with other pilots to take off for the "Battle of Britain Day" anniversary.

sequence of events. The main characters were a pilot, Flt Lt Neil Cox DFC from No 53 OTU, Spitfire Mark VB serial number AB910, and a WAAF ground crew fitter, LACW Margaret Horton. In difficult windy conditions, Cox started his engine and taxied his aircraft to the run-up point near the runway;

► Pilots of the Free French Spitfire Squadron running to their planes.

LACW Horton was following the customary practice of acting as human ballast, by lying across the leading edge of the tailplane, in order to prevent the

aircraft nosing-over at high power while stationary. On completion of his engine functional check, the pilot taxied to the take-off point and, without realising that his human ballast was still present, commenced his take-off run. Cox soon noticed that the usually sensitive pitch control of the Spitfire had become exceptionally heavy and completed a, thankfully, brief circuit and landed safely, without any undue harm befalling his unwitting passenger. The aircraft involved, AB910, having first been delivered to the RAF in August 1941, is still flying today with the BBMF.

As one of the most highly-developed aircraft in RAF history, the Spitfire has appeared in many guises with a variety of weapons, both internal and external, and many appendages such as floats, skis, catapult attachments, and tail hooks: one extraordinary proposed modification was intended to enable this single-seat fighter to carry two passengers in addition to its pilot. In 1943, the Station Commander of RAF Biggin Hill, Group Captain Barwell, put forward a modification that would provide for the carriage of two people, one on each wing, of a Spitfire. The modification involved the use of a canvas-type

▶ A Spitfire LF Mark IX with a name dedication painted on the side.

material being fashioned into a shape that bore a remarkable resemblance to that of a body-bag! One of these bags was placed on top of each wing, and secured with a loop at its forward end being passed around the cannon barrel fairing; the rear end was fastened to the wing structure forward of the flap. It was not documented as having been tested with a live passenger.

Following on from a long-standing British tradition, dating back to the days of the Crusades, of presenting warriors with weapons and armour, the donation of a gift of military hardware became commonplace during WW1, when tanks and aircraft were donated by wealthy benefactors. This tradition was maintained throughout the inter-war years and into WW2: gift items usually bore the name of the donor in recognition of their generosity. In many circumstances, the aircraft or, exceptionally, the squadron that had been gifted, was itself renamed in honour of the donor, as in No 152 (Hyderabad) Squadron of the RAF, after his donation of a whole squadron by the Nizam of Hyderabad. A representation of the Nizam's turban head-dress forms the centrepiece of that squadron's

official badge.

Lord Beaverbrook was a particularly strong advocate of public donation

towards Britain's war effort. Whether this was purely a propaganda exercise, or a practical means of providing a worthwhile contribution to the production of aircraft is arguable; his 1940 appeal to the public, calling for

them to support production of the Spitfire by donating their household aluminium pots and pans, as well as sums of money, was well-received and the response, magnificent.

For the purpose of Lord Beaverbrook's scheme, the price of a Spitfire was a nominal £5,000, although the true cost was around £12,000. Many towns, cities and organisations, as well as some individuals, all having donated the necessary sum, were recognised by their name or fund title being applied in four-inch high letters, in yellow, on the fuselage of "their" aircraft. Occasionally, the actual name-plate style was somewhat different from that of the official version. Such was the success of the donation scheme that it has been calculated that around 1,500 Spitfires were presented in this way. The name-plate tradition has been revived by the present-day No 72 Squadron, two of their Tucano training aircraft being named "City of Leeds" and "Wings of Victory" after donated Spitfires.

The Spitfire lives on: it is now technically possible to manufacture a complete aircraft from scratch, such is the knowledge and expertise of those

◄ A Spitfire flies over Duxford Aerodrome in Cambridgeshire.

▶ The "Sentinel" near the former Spitfire factory in Castle Bromwich.

who have dedicated their lives to the unbelievably expensive restoration and, in some cases, the total rebuild of many examples of this iconic aircraft. It is also possible to purchase a flyable, 80 percent scale replica Spitfire, of which there are around 30 flying worldwide. For those considering the purchase of a Spitfire, be it a replica or the real thing, be warned, as for all things Spitfire, it will be expensive! The main limitation to the production of an *authentic* new-build Spitfire is in the engine department. Unlike the flyable scale-version that uses a car engine, there are few suitable power plants available for the full-size version. The Merlin, in any condition, is highly sought after, as is the Griffon. The "power" and the "growler" are in their element when performing their distinctive repertoire, and all airworthy examples have their flying hours carefully monitored so that the almost legendary aircraft, the Spitfire, can be kept flying, thus paying tribute to those who created, flew, and maintained her. Her place in history is assured, not only as a beautiful and effective fighting machine, but also as a symbol of hope for a nation in the dark years of conflict.

Other books also available:

  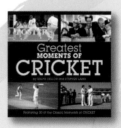 

   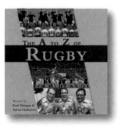

Available from all major stockists

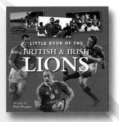

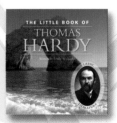

Available from all major stockists

The pictures in this book were provided courtesy of the following:

GETTY IMAGES
101 Bayham Street, London NW1 0AG

PA PHOTOS
www.paphotos.com

Creative Director: Kevin Gardner

Design and Artwork: Jane Stephens

Picture research: Ellie Charleston

Published by Green Umbrella Publishing

Publishers Jules Gammond and Vanessa Gardner

Written by David Curnock

I L♦VE
THE
TUDORS

First published 2016.

Pitkin Publishing
The History Press
The Mill, Brimscombe Port
Stroud, Gloucestershire GL5 2QG
www.thehistorypress.co.uk

Enquiries and sales: 01453 883300
Email: sales@thehistorypress.co.uk

Text written by Mickey Mayhew.
The author has asserted their moral rights.

Designed by Chris West.

British Library Cataloguing in Publication Data.
A Catalogue record for this book is available from the British Library.

Publication in this form © Pitkin Publishing 2016.

ISBN 978-1-84165-697-7 1/16

*To Shaminder Takhar
and Jenny Owen,
for endless patience
and Tudor chit–chat.*

Contents

Facts

CHAPTER ONE: Henry VII   1 – 14

CHAPTER TWO: Henry VIII   15 – 217

CHAPTER THREE: Edward VI   218 – 227

CHAPTER FOUR: Lady Jane Grey   228 – 237

CHAPTER FIVE: 'Bloody' Mary   238 – 260

CHAPTER SIX: Elizabeth I   261 – 400

CHAPTER ONE

Henry VII

1 Henry VII, the founder of the Tudor dynasty, justified his seizure of the Crown on the grounds that God alone had decided his victory at the Battle of Bosworth.

2 Henry's mother, Margaret Beaufort, was only thirteen when she gave birth to him in January 1457.

3 Henry VII spent his early years living in exile in France; his lineage made him a danger to the Crown.

4 Henry's father, Edmund Tudor, 1st Earl of Richmond, died in prison three months before Henry VII was born.

5 As punishment for pretending to be the Earl of Warwick, Lambert Simnel was sent to work in the kitchens by Henry VII. He grew up there, married and had children, one of whom became a monk.

6 Perkin Warbeck (pictured), who claimed to be one of the vanished Princes in the Tower and who was executed on the 23 November 1499 for trying to con both king and country, may actually have been related to the boys: it's possible that he was one of the king's illegitimate children, and that Edward IV really was his father.

7 In a strange coincidence, the heirs of both Henry VII and Henry VIII died when they were fifteen.

8 Later residents of Eltham Palace, where Henry VII's children were for the main part raised, included a pet lemur called Mah-Jongg who lived in his own bedroom at the top of the house.

9 Today, the main hall is the only Tudor section of Eltham Palace that remains.

10 Catherine of Aragon was married to Henry VII's son Prince Arthur before she married his brother Henry VIII.

11 Before the marriage between Catherine and Prince Arthur was agreed, the prince was stripped and inspected for the benefit of the Spanish Ambassador.

12 The Ambassador then represented Catherine at a proxy wedding ceremony, solemnly taking Prince Arthur's hand during the vows. The two men then enjoyed Catherine's proxy wedding feast together.

13 Henry VIII was not the only Tudor interested in marrying Catherine of Aragon: after Prince Arthur's death, she narrowly escaped being married to her father-in-law, Henry VII.

14 Henry VII was fifty-two years old when he died. His reign had lasted for almost twenty-four years.

CHAPTER TWO

Henry VIII

15 Henry VIII was a towering Tudor: in an age when the average height of a man was a mere 5ft 8in, Henry was a majestic 6ft 1in – some accounts say as tall as 6ft 3in.

16 Catherine of Aragon, far from being the dark, demur wife of film and TV, was in fact a flame-haired, non-stereotypical Spanish beauty, small, and in later years somewhat stout.

17 Annette Crosby's Catherine in the 1970 BBC series *The Six Wives of Henry VIII* is one of the very few examples of Catherine being portrayed with the correct colouring.

18 Henry and Catherine of Aragon's marriage lasted nearly twenty-four years – you could fit his other five marriages, twice over, into that same timeframe.

19 As well as competitive sports such as jousting, court entertainments during Henry VIII's reign included more surprising acts such as performing monkeys.

20 The diet of the nobility consisted almost exclusively of meat and fish; vegetables were considered to be mainly for the consumption of the poor.

21 The court menu included swan, goose, peacock, venison, lark and heron.

22 People mostly drank beer or wine: water was simply too dirty to consume.

23 Even Tudor children drank beer. However, Tudor beer was far weaker than today's brew.

24 There were no forks in Tudor times. People used knives and fingers to eat; the nobility used finger bowls full of scented water to wash their hands during meals.

25

The sort of bread you could afford to eat said a lot about your social standing: the rich ate white wholemeal, while the poor put up with rye and sometimes ate ground acorns.

   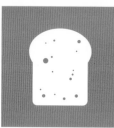 

26

Puddings decorated with marzipan came in all shapes and sizes, and were made into little animals, buildings, or other such fare to grace the table at the end of a meal. Honey was often used to sweeten things as it was cheaper than sugar.

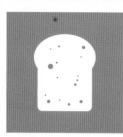 

27

There was no 'lunch' in Tudor times: dinner, the main meal of the day, was served at around 11 a.m.

28 Breakfast was even earlier, sometimes as early as 6 a.m.

29 Supper was at what we now consider to be a 'traditional' dinner-time, i.e. around 5 p.m.

30 Whilst Henry was away warring in France, Catherine – co-ordinating matters on the home front from London – helped to repulse a Scottish invasion. She then offered to send the head of the dead king James IV to Henry in France. Disappointingly, she was told that the very idea was barbaric in the extreme.

31 Lady Blount was a courtier of considerable beauty. She was also Henry VIII's mistress for several years, and gave Henry the son he longed for. However, because he was illegitimate Henry VIII's son with 'Bessie' Blount could not claim the throne.

32 Henry had a secret house in Essex called 'Jericho', where he and Lady Blount met for their little dalliances.

33 Henry VIII's illegitimate son was named Henry Fitzroy; 'Fitzroy' means 'son of the king'.

34 According to one theory, Anne Boleyn (pictured), Henry's 'scandalous' second wife, may in fact have been Henry VIII's own daughter: rumours of an affair with Anne's mother were rife in the Tudor court, and persisted for centuries afterwards.

35 Mary Boleyn, another of Henry's mistresses, was either Anne Boleyn's older or younger sister: because the dates of their births were not recorded, historians have continued to struggle with this.

36 Mary Boleyn was once called 'the great whore' or 'the great prostitute' because of her alleged dalliances with, among others, the King of France. Since Philippa Gregory's novel *The Other Boleyn Girl*, however, she has become a major player in Tudor studies.

37 Anne Boleyn most likely didn't have six fingers on one hand: an examination of skeletons exhumed in the chapel of St Peter ad Vincula (where she is buried) during Victorian times found none with such an abnormality.

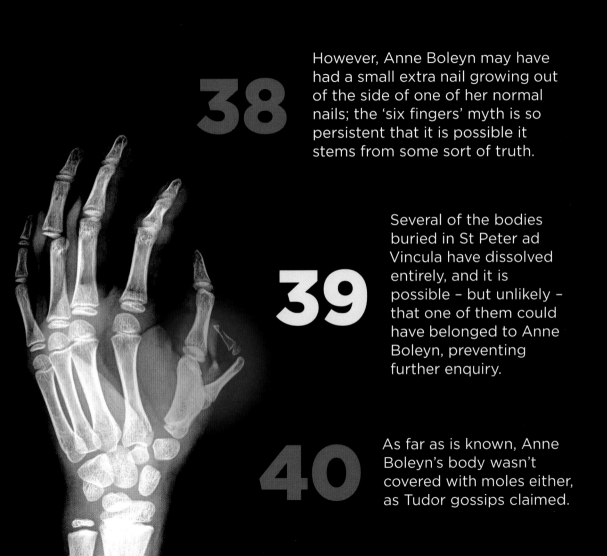

38 However, Anne Boleyn may have had a small extra nail growing out of the side of one of her normal nails; the 'six fingers' myth is so persistent that it is possible it stems from some sort of truth.

39 Several of the bodies buried in St Peter ad Vincula have dissolved entirely, and it is possible – but unlikely – that one of them could have belonged to Anne Boleyn, preventing further enquiry.

40 As far as is known, Anne Boleyn's body wasn't covered with moles either, as Tudor gossips claimed.

41 Nor did Anne Boleyn have a huge growth hanging from her throat.

42 It is quite possible, however, that Anne Boleyn was on one occasion chased out of a house on the Strand by a mob of angry women and forced to flee onto a boat, taking to the Thames to escape the fury they felt at the king's treatment of Catherine of Aragon.

43 Scotland Yard may derive its name from the fact that Margaret Tudor, Henry's sister (who had married James IV), took up residence in part of a palace now on the present site, along with her Scottish retinue; before that it was often used to accommodate Scottish diplomats.

44 Cardinal Wolsey (pictured), Henry's chief advisor for most of the early part of his reign, rose to greatness despite being nothing more than the humble son of an Ipswich butcher.

45 Today there is a statue of Cardinal Wolsey in his home town, and people often leave empty lager cans in his outstretched hand as a sort of tribute.

46 Cardinal Wolsey gave his palace at Hampton Court to the king as a way of currying favour; Wolsey lived as well as, if not slightly better, than Henry himself, and accusations of indulgence played a part in his eventual downfall.

47 The astronomical clock at Hampton Court was built by Nicholas Oursian and tells, among other things, the time of high tide at London Bridge, a very important fact when most commutes were made by boat (or royal barge).

48 The traditional black and white timber buildings erected by the Tudors proved so popular that their design is still used today (known, of course, as 'mock Tudor').

49 Tudor roofs were covered with thatch, or sometimes with tiles. These houses were made of wood, and were thus extremely flammable: the fact that the Great Fire didn't happen until 1666 was something of a miracle.

50 Many Tudor words were different from those we use today; for instance, virginity in Tudor times was referred to as 'maidenhead' or 'maidenhood'.

51 Talking of maidenhood, Henry VIII was the king who repealed the death penalty for lecherous priests.

52 The meeting of the kings of England and of France at the Field of the Cloth of Gold in 1520 cost Henry VIII as much as £13,000, an astronomical sum at the time.

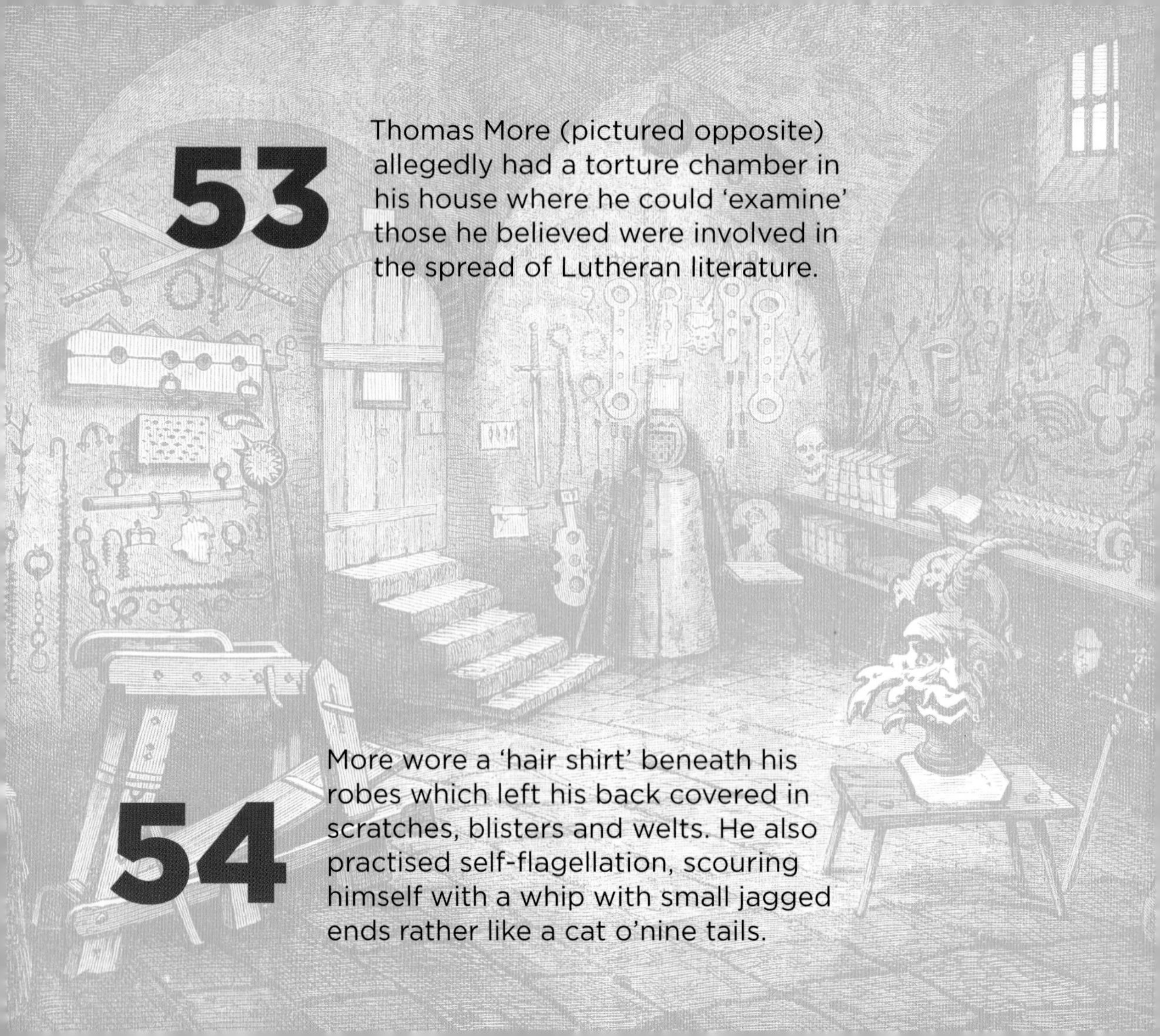

53 Thomas More (pictured opposite) allegedly had a torture chamber in his house where he could 'examine' those he believed were involved in the spread of Lutheran literature.

54 More wore a 'hair shirt' beneath his robes which left his back covered in scratches, blisters and welts. He also practised self-flagellation, scouring himself with a whip with small jagged ends rather like a cat o'nine tails.

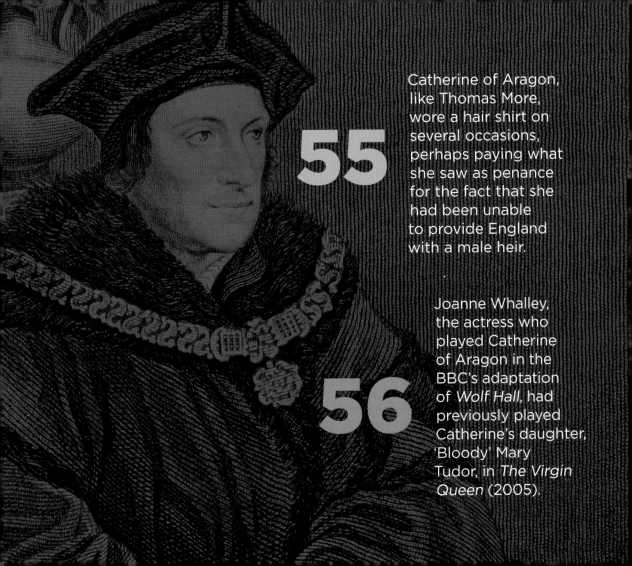

55

Catherine of Aragon, like Thomas More, wore a hair shirt on several occasions, perhaps paying what she saw as penance for the fact that she had been unable to provide England with a male heir.

56

Joanne Whalley, the actress who played Catherine of Aragon in the BBC's adaptation of *Wolf Hall*, had previously played Catherine's daughter, 'Bloody' Mary Tudor, in *The Virgin Queen* (2005).

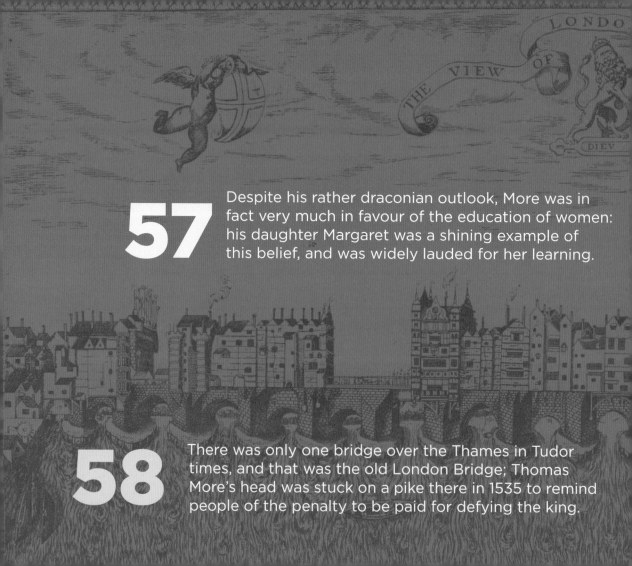

57 Despite his rather draconian outlook, More was in fact very much in favour of the education of women: his daughter Margaret was a shining example of this belief, and was widely lauded for her learning.

58 There was only one bridge over the Thames in Tudor times, and that was the old London Bridge; Thomas More's head was stuck on a pike there in 1535 to remind people of the penalty to be paid for defying the king.

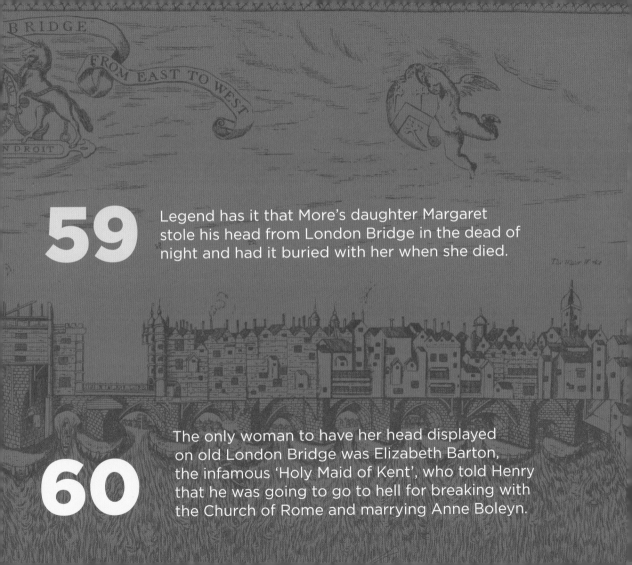

59 Legend has it that More's daughter Margaret stole his head from London Bridge in the dead of night and had it buried with her when she died.

60 The only woman to have her head displayed on old London Bridge was Elizabeth Barton, the infamous 'Holy Maid of Kent', who told Henry that he was going to go to hell for breaking with the Church of Rome and marrying Anne Boleyn.

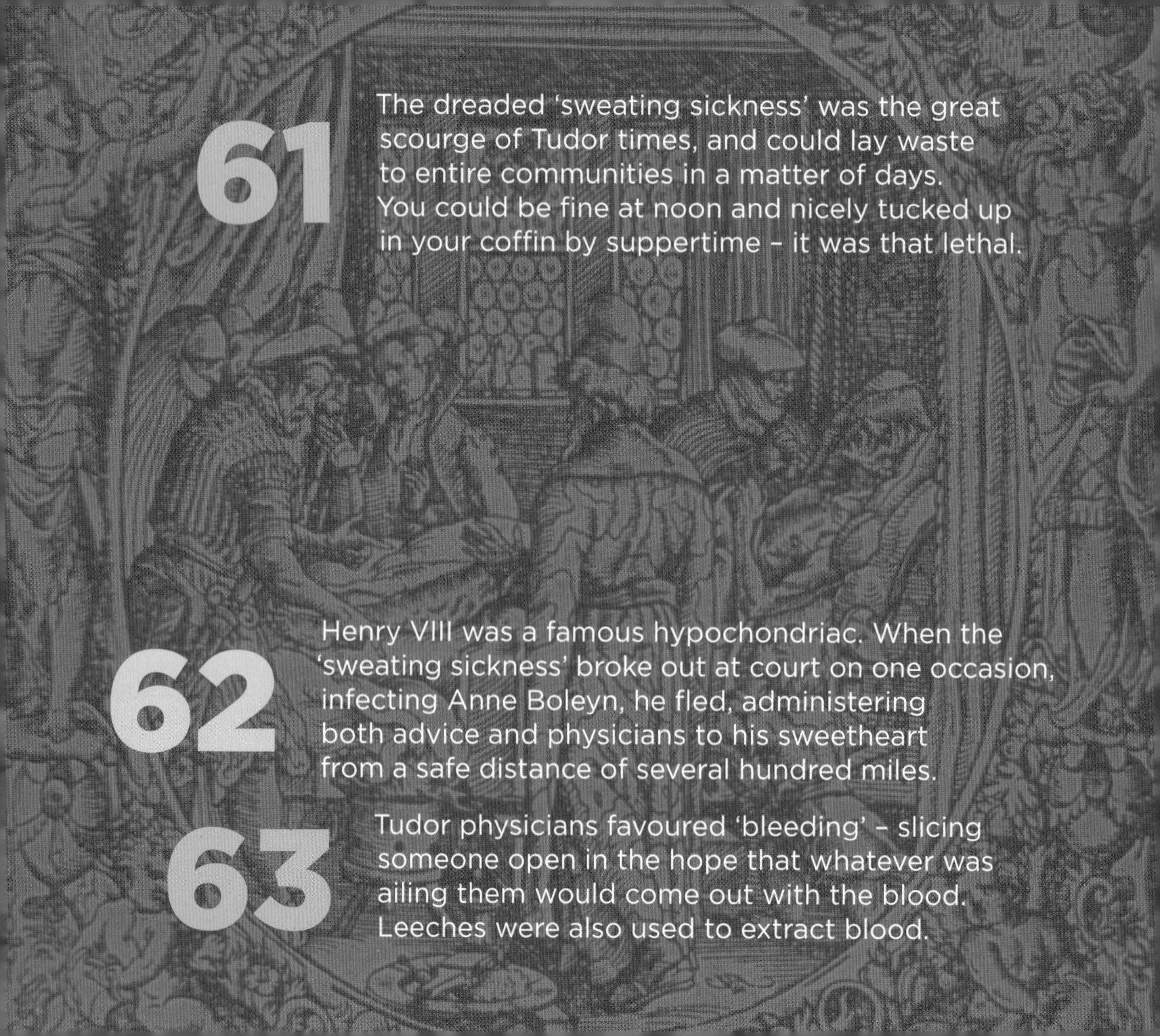

61

The dreaded 'sweating sickness' was the great scourge of Tudor times, and could lay waste to entire communities in a matter of days. You could be fine at noon and nicely tucked up in your coffin by suppertime – it was that lethal.

62

Henry VIII was a famous hypochondriac. When the 'sweating sickness' broke out at court on one occasion, infecting Anne Boleyn, he fled, administering both advice and physicians to his sweetheart from a safe distance of several hundred miles.

63

Tudor physicians favoured 'bleeding' – slicing someone open in the hope that whatever was ailing them would come out with the blood. Leeches were also used to extract blood.

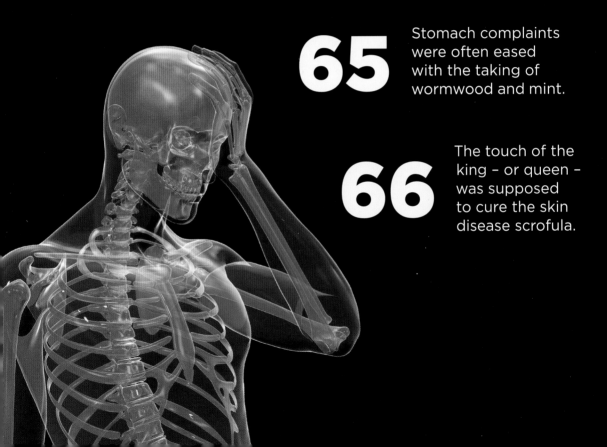

64 Tudor headaches were treated using herbs such as lavender and sage.

65 Stomach complaints were often eased with the taking of wormwood and mint.

66 The touch of the king – or queen – was supposed to cure the skin disease scrofula.

67 Disease forced many people into poverty. However, you had to have a license to beg, and failure to produce one could lead to a severe flogging.

68 Desperate measures were often taken to reduce the spread of the various deadly diseases during Tudor times, one of which was to seal an entire inflicted household within their walls for up to six weeks, so that they could 'sweat' it out on their own.

69 Smallpox was much feared by the Tudors: Elizabeth I caught it, and so did Mary Queen of Scots.

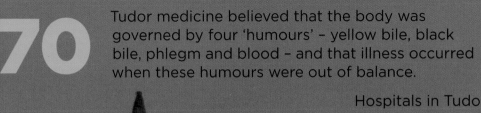

70 Tudor medicine believed that the body was governed by four 'humours' – yellow bile, black bile, phlegm and blood – and that illness occurred when these humours were out of balance.

71 Hospitals in Tudor times were run by monasteries, another reason the Dissolution of the Monasteries by Henry and Thomas Cromwell was so unpopular.

72 George Boleyn, Anne's beloved brother, was the governor of the Bethlem Hospital (or 'Bedlam'), the famous hospital for the insane; in Tudor times this was located near modern-day Liverpool Street station in the City of London.

73 Diseases spread easily because hygiene and sanitation were so bad. Tudors thought nothing of relieving themselves in the street, and this went as much for the monarchy as it did for the common folk.

74 Peeing in public was helped by the fact that the floors of most palaces were strewn with 'rushes' or straw mats; peeing on a rare and expensive Turkey carpet would have been far more unforgivable.

75 If you didn't slip in urine then you might end up showered in it, as people pouring their unwanted waste out of their windows was a common hazard on your average Tudor street.

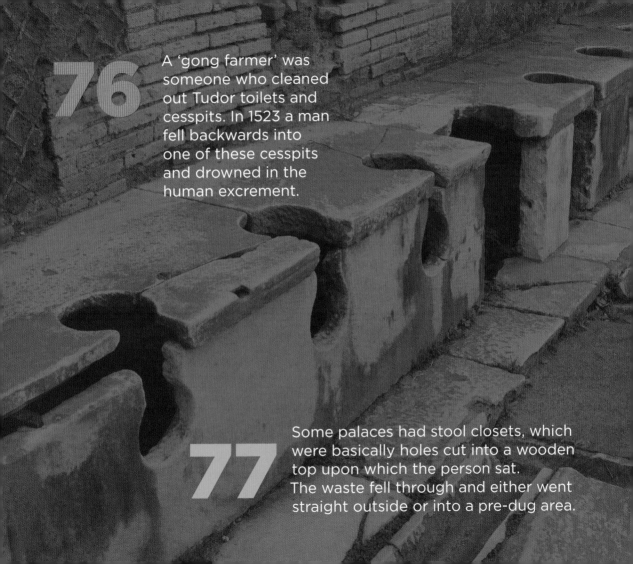

76 A 'gong farmer' was someone who cleaned out Tudor toilets and cesspits. In 1523 a man fell backwards into one of these cesspits and drowned in the human excrement.

77 Some palaces had stool closets, which were basically holes cut into a wooden top upon which the person sat. The waste fell through and either went straight outside or into a pre-dug area.

78 John Harington was the inventor of what would be considered the first flushing toilet. Henry VIII's daughter Elizabeth I was so taken with the invention that she had one installed in 1596.

79 There was no toilet roll: if you were rich you used cloth to clean yourself, which was washed and then used again; if you were poor, however, you had to make do with a fistful of leaves or whatever else came to hand.

80 There are no records of sanitary towels either: reusable clothes were probably employed for this function in much the same way as they were for toilet roll.

81 Tudors believed that women's wombs could move all over their bodies, pressing themselves against various organs and causing all sorts of ailments. This was called 'wandering womb' syndrome.

82

Henry re-founded Christ Church College in Oxford in 1546, originally conceived by Cardinal Wolsey.

83 Henry could be two-faced on an industrial scale; when Wolsey failed to secure his divorce from Rome Henry greeted him like a long-lost friend one day and then rode off the next on the hunt, never to see him again.

84 Henry was to behave in roughly the same manner with both Anne Boleyn's father and also Thomas Cromwell shortly before their respective downfalls.

85 Bishop John Fisher was a staunch opponent of Henry's divorce. At one point an (unsuccessful) attempt was made to poison him: nothing has been proved, but the Boleyn family are of course significant suspects.

86 Henry acted swiftly, though, making sure that the poor cook who had prepared the poisoned food was boiled alive in oil.

87 Bishop Fisher was made a cardinal by Rome for opposing Henry's marriage to Anne Boleyn; in response, Henry declared that Fisher would have no need of the hat without his head. He had Fisher executed.

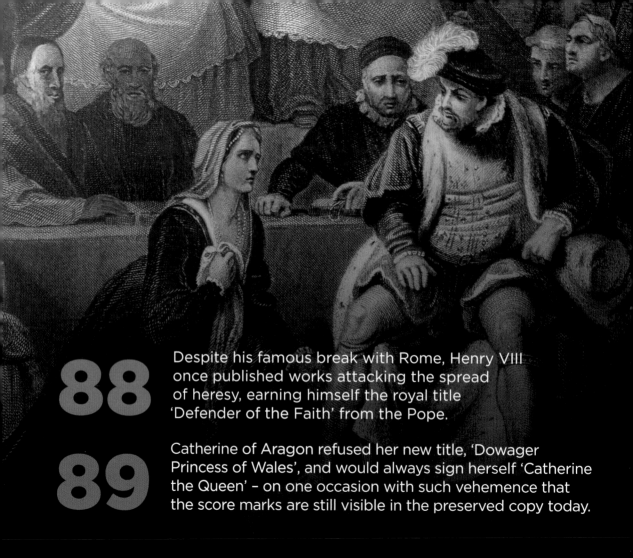

88 Despite his famous break with Rome, Henry VIII once published works attacking the spread of heresy, earning himself the royal title 'Defender of the Faith' from the Pope.

89 Catherine of Aragon refused her new title, 'Dowager Princess of Wales', and would always sign herself 'Catherine the Queen' – on one occasion with such vehemence that the score marks are still visible in the preserved copy today.

90 Anne Boleyn and Henry's entwined initials were 'HA', a rather unfortunate confluence which caused the crowds at her coronation no end of amusement.

91 When Anne was executed, Henry ordered all their entwined 'HA' monograms be removed. Somehow two extremely prominent examples still survive in Hampton Court Palace to this day, one of them in the Great Hall.

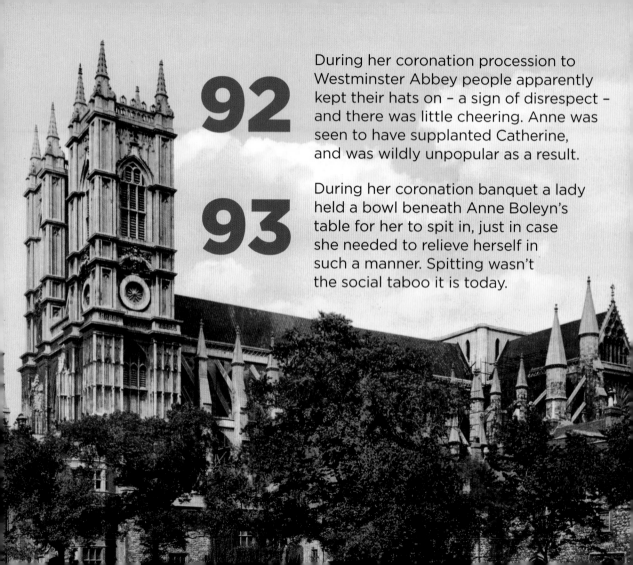

92

During her coronation procession to Westminster Abbey people apparently kept their hats on – a sign of disrespect – and there was little cheering. Anne was seen to have supplanted Catherine, and was wildly unpopular as a result.

93

During her coronation banquet a lady held a bowl beneath Anne Boleyn's table for her to spit in, just in case she needed to relieve herself in such a manner. Spitting wasn't the social taboo it is today.

94 Henry and Anne Boleyn's marriage lasted for just under three and a half years. Apart from his first wife, only Catherine Parr lasted longer.

95 The West Ham football ground is called the Boleyn Ground because Anne Boleyn is believed to have owned or stayed in a house nearby; chemists, retailers and cinemas nearby also bear her name.

96 Anne Boleyn's pregnancy was portrayed on *The Simpsons*: her cartoon self carried the slogan 'a son'll come out – tomorrow'!

97 Anne Boleyn gave birth to Elizabeth I at Greenwich Palace, of which now almost nothing remains.

98 Anne would also be arrested at Greenwich Palace some three years later, and conveyed by barge to the Tower of London.

99 As part of what was called her 'lying-in', Anne Boleyn was confined to a darkened room for several weeks leading up to the birth of the future Queen Elizabeth I.

100 Mary Tudor's recalcitrance where her father's new marriage was concerned so incensed Anne Boleyn that she remarked that the girl should have her ears boxed, 'like the cursed bastard that she was'.

101 Anne Boleyn had a dog called Purkoy, whom she loved dearly – and who either fell out of a window by chance, or was slung henceforth by a disgruntled Catholic courtier.

102 She also had a greyhound called Urian. He was not named after Satan, as some Catholic propagandists have suggested, but after a courtier called Urian Brereton, brother of Sir William, one of the men beheaded for allegedly having had intimate relations with the queen.

103

One pet Anne didn't have was a monkey, because she reportedly loathed them; perhaps this was something to do with the fact that Catherine of Aragon loved the little blighters, and even had one sit with her for one of her portraits.

104

Whilst dogs were popular pets in Tudor times, cats were most certainly not.

105 When Catherine of Aragon died, both Henry and Anne were said to have decked themselves out in bright yellow, an act which many found quite shocking. However, yellow was in fact the colour of mourning in Spain.

106 Some historians have – by their own admission – become so besotted with Anne Boleyn that they've taken to making pot-shots about her successor Jane Seymour's appearance.

107 It took Anne Boleyn eight years of hard graft to get the crown of England on her head. Employing roughly the same tactics, Jane Seymour fast-tracked her own success down to a mere matter of months.

108

Jane Seymour's family home was called 'Wolf Hall', later used as the title for Hilary Mantel's best-selling novel of the same name.

109

Henry was touchy about his reproductive abilities, bursting out on one occasion, 'Am I not a man like other men? Am I not? Am I not?' within earshot of his astonished courtiers.

110 Anne Boleyn was accused of adultery with seven men, but court rumour held that she had in fact taken 'hundreds' of lovers.

111 Musician Mark Smeaton was most likely racked as a result of his possible liaison with Anne Boleyn, torture having become the Tudor 'go to' method for making someone confess.

112 Racking meant tying a victim to a board with ropes secured around wrists and ankles, a pulley system operating the whole thing at either end. Dislocations were inevitable. As an extra torment, a bucket of cold water was often thrown on the victim's face to revive them when they passed out from the pain.

113 The rack was so feared that some people had only to be shown it to confess to their guilt – even if they were actually innocent.

114 There was also a dungeon in the Tower called 'Little Ease', just 4ft square all around.

115 The manacles were considered a more merciful form of torture, the victim dangled by the wrists for hours at a time. However, the flesh swelled so badly that victims were still liable to faint from the pain when the manacles were removed.

116 Of all the men accused of adultery with Anne Boleyn, Mark Smeaton was the only one to maintain his guilt right up to the point of his death...

117 ...which may have been the reason Mary Tudor sometimes insisted he was half-sister Elizabeth's real father, despite Elizabeth's obvious inheritance of Henry VIII's famous flaming red hair.

118 George Boleyn, Anne's beloved brother, was accused of incest by his own wife, Lady Jane Rochford.

119 Clearly the marriage of George Boleyn and Lady Rochford wasn't a happy one. This has led some to speculate that George may have been homosexual, and even that Mark Smeaton had been one of his lovers.

120 The Act against buggery was first passed in 1533, the year Henry married Anne Boleyn. Somewhat surprisingly, 'Bloody' Mary Tudor repealed it, but Elizabeth I had it reinstated.

121

Poet Thomas Wyatt
(pictured) was another
man accused of
committing adultery
with Anne Boleyn.
He may have been her
lover in bygone days,
possibly making a
reference to her (as a
mystery 'brunette')
in one of his poems.

122 Anne Boleyn was executed on Tower Green on 19 May 1536; Henry was being merciful when he allowed her to be decapitated using a sword rather than the axe.

123 The historian Alison Weir nevertheless cites the work of two French doctors, who described the method of decapitation, by axe or by sword, as a 'savage vivisection' whereby every element of the body survives the initial beheading for seconds, even minutes.

124 No coffin had been provided for Anne's body, so she was instead put into an old arrow chest which had been lying nearby.

125 Henry and Jane Seymour tactfully waited a full day after Anne's execution before being betrothed.

126 Henry and Jane Seymour's marriage lasted less than eighteen months.

127 Jane favoured the gable hood, the hallmark of Catherine of Aragon, as opposed to the French hood favoured by Anne Boleyn.

128 Anne's ghost reportedly haunts the church of St Peter and St Paul, in the village of Salle, Norfolk, resting place of her ancestors, in the form of a 'great hare'...

129 ...as well as the lawns of her home at Hever Castle, and what is believed to have been her birthplace of Blickling Hall in Norfolk.

130 Her father is also supposed to haunt Blickling, along with a headless coachman driving a coach of headless horses.

131 Anne Boleyn also haunts Hampton Court, but top creepy kudos in that department go to Catherine Howard – Henry's fifth wife – and her ghost, whose mad dash for mercy in what is now known as the 'Haunted Gallery' has apparently caused some visitors to faint from shock.

132 Jane Seymour's ghost is also said to haunt Hampton Court, walking around the grounds looking for her son before disappearing into the building to find him. The room where she gave birth is no longer accessible to the public and is now used as a place for actors to change their costumes.

133 William Packenham Walsh, a canon of Peterborough Cathedral, claimed to have held séances in the 1960s where he spoke to Anne Boleyn, and to Henry as well.

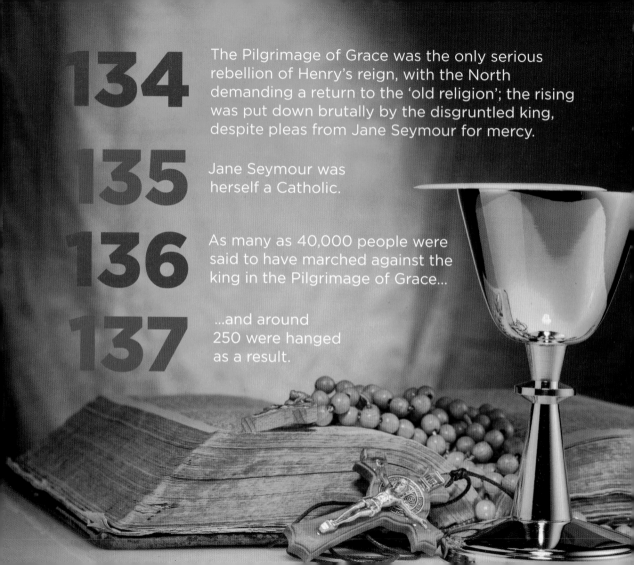

134 The Pilgrimage of Grace was the only serious rebellion of Henry's reign, with the North demanding a return to the 'old religion'; the rising was put down brutally by the disgruntled king, despite pleas from Jane Seymour for mercy.

135 Jane Seymour was herself a Catholic.

136 As many as 40,000 people were said to have marched against the king in the Pilgrimage of Grace...

137 ...and around 250 were hanged as a result.

138

When Jane Seymour was pregnant she developed a craving for quail's eggs, large numbers of which were duly shipped to England for her delectation.

139

Edward VI, Henry's longed-for heir, was born on 12 October 1537, but the triumph was tarnished with tragedy when his mother succumbed to 'childbed fever'.

140

Jane Seymour was the only one of Henry's six wives to receive a queen's funeral, though Mary I later buried Anne of Cleves with all due ceremony.

141 Henry spent his longest time as a single man after Jane Seymour's death, whilst Thomas Cromwell busied himself by scouring the European circuit for a suitable bride. There weren't many takers for the king's hand.

142 Marriage in Tudor times was a lot less about love and a lot more about uniting families and keeping hold of properties. 'Love matches' were rare.

143 It was also during this time that Henry undertook his most magnificent building project, erecting the fairytale palace of Nonsuch in Surrey. Just a few slabs of building work and a marker with a plaque remain today.

144 Henry and his father built or renovated many palaces, but his children didn't build any.

145 Nor did they bother to put up for him the great tomb Henry VIII had planned in Windsor Castle.

146 The population of England and Wales by the middle of Henry's reign was around 2.4 million.

147 Lady Ursula Misseldon, a character in the TV show *The Tudors*, is entirely fictional. However, she may be based on an unidentified mistress from the time of Henry's marriage to Anne Boleyn: Henry apparently claimed, in the early days of his marriage to Jane Seymour, that he wished he'd married someone else.

148 Anne of Cleves (pictured), Henry VIII's fourth wife, was about as close to internet dating at the Tudors got: Henry agreed to marry her on the basis of her portrait.

149 Henry famously dismissed Anne as the 'Flanders Mare' when she arrived. However, by this time Henry was fat and the ulcer on his leg, by all accounts, stank terribly: in truth, she may in fact have rejected him.

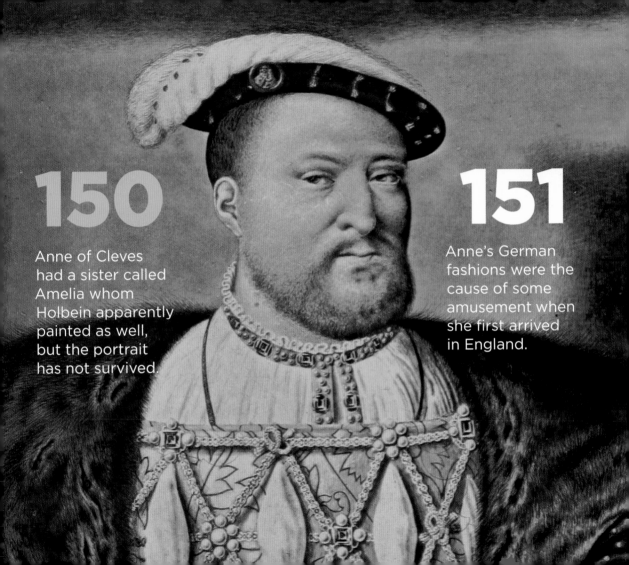

150

Anne of Cleves had a sister called Amelia whom Holbein apparently painted as well, but the portrait has not survived.

151

Anne's German fashions were the cause of some amusement when she first arrived in England.

152

153

154

Feminist historians have speculated that Anne of Cleves may have been a lesbian, and that she actively rebuffed the king's advances; the fact that she never remarried or took a male companion in the subsequent seventeen years of her life in England following the annulment of her marriage to Henry adds some weight to this argument.

Henry and Anne of Cleves' marriage was the shortest of all his matches, lasting for a mere six months and three days.

Although the English were – and some might say still are – famously xenophobic, both Henry's foreign queens, Catherine of Aragon and Anne of Cleves, were well loved by the public.

155

The famous portrait of Henry VIII with legs splayed and hands on hips was painted around this time, and his courtiers were quick to ape the wide-shouldered, codpieced look.

156

By the time his daughter Elizabeth I had ascended to the throne, the look – on all fronts – had died a death, and fashions for men became slightly more 'dainty'.

157

Thomas Cromwell lost his head for his arrangement of the disastrous Cleves marriage. If you believe *The Tudors* TV series, Cromwell was so loathed that various nobles conspired to get the executioner drunk the night before: as a result, Cromwell was almost hacked to death before a dutiful guard proceeded to behead what was left of his body.

158

Oliver Cromwell, Thomas Cromwell's descendant, executed Charles I and became Lord Protector of England a little over 100 years after Thomas's death.

159

Beheadings were reserved for the nobility: most criminals were hanged, and traitors were hanged, drawn, and quartered.

160

People could be hanged in Tudor times for something as simple as theft. However, petty treason – killing a superior, usually a husband or master – meant a much more horrible death: burning at the stake.

161

Cardinal Reginald Pole, a descendant of Edward III who had written various tracts against Henry, fled to the Continent, so Henry made do with executing his mother instead. Poor Margaret Pole fled from the axe and had to be chased around Tower Green, with the executioner taking fevered swipes at her neck.

162

Catherine Howard, Henry VIII's fifth wife, was his mid-life crisis; she was just a teenager, perhaps as young as sixteen, whilst Henry was well into his forties when they married.

163 Catherine was apparently so curvaceous that Henry couldn't keep his hands off her, even in public: the incidents are well recorded. How much Catherine enjoyed being groped by a bloated old lecher was not recorded.

164 Before she married Henry, Catherine Howard was a maid-of-waiting – to Anne of Cleves! Catherine was also related to Anne Boleyn: she was her cousin.

165 Anne of Cleves harboured no ill-feelings towards her successor: they even danced together at Christmas, a first for two of Henry's wives.

166

Thomas Culpeper, with whom Catherine became rather taken, was a gentleman of Henry's Privy chamber, but he was also possibly a rapist (though the offence may have been committed by his brother, who shared the name). Either way, Henry pardoned the Culpeper responsible for the attack on a park-keeper's wife.

167

Lady Rochford, aka Jane Boleyn, had continued to serve under Henry's queens after George Boleyn's death, but she came a cropper with Catherine Howard. For reasons that have baffled historians for hundreds of years, Jane acted as a bawd for the young queen and Thomas Culpeper. If you believe *The Tudors* TV series, she did it because because she enjoyed watching the couple together, making her the Tudor equivalent of a Peeping Tom.

168 Henry was rather fond of Thomas Culpeper – 'a beautiful youth' – so he had his sentence commuted to a simple beheading.

169 Most executions – including those of Culpeper and Dereham – took place at Tyburn, very close to what is now Marble Arch in London, and most of the bodies were thrown into a nearby pit afterwards.

170 Culpeper, however, escaped this fate; he is buried in St Sepulchre-without-Newgate church in London, just along from High Holborn.

171

During his marriage to Catherine Howard, Henry embarked on his biggest 'progress', visiting Lincoln and York (pictured), among other places. Progresses were the Tudor way of letting the people see their king.

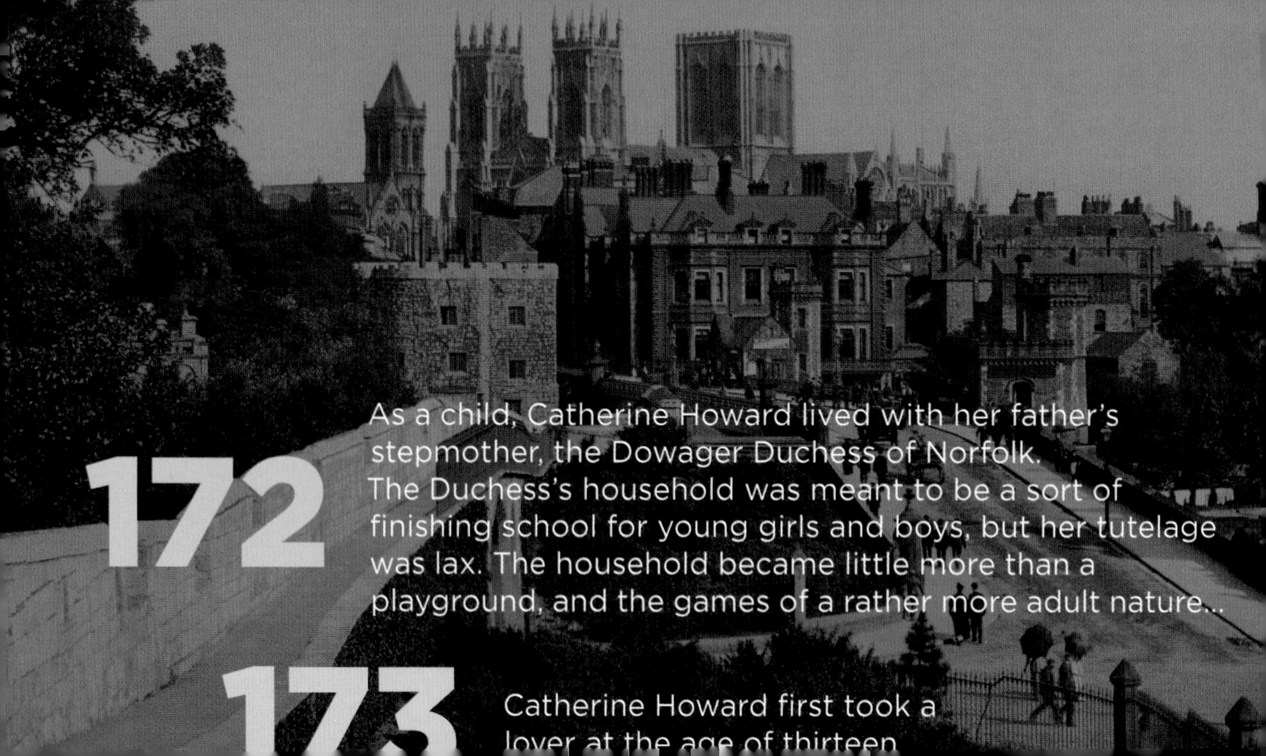

172

As a child, Catherine Howard lived with her father's stepmother, the Dowager Duchess of Norfolk. The Duchess's household was meant to be a sort of finishing school for young girls and boys, but her tutelage was lax. The household became little more than a playground, and the games of a rather more adult nature...

173

Catherine Howard first took a lover at the age of thirteen.

174

Francis Dereham was a former lover of Catherine Howard's who returned to her service when she became queen, an extremely unwise move given Henry's famous Tudor temper: he was hanged, drawn and quartered for having 'spoiled' Catherine for the king.

175

Lady Rochford went mad after being imprisoned in the Tower of London for her involvement in the affair.

176

There was no law to sanction the execution of a mad person, so Henry simply had one drawn up: she was beheaded with her queen on Tower Green.

177

For many years it was not known which grave in St Peter ad Vincula belonged to Catherine Howard, which to Lady Rochford and which to Anne Boleyn.

178 Baynard's Castle, sitting on the north bank of the Thames just down from Blackfriars and given to Catherine Howard by the king, is now a BT office.

179 Executions were among the best outdoor entertainment to be had in Tudor times: people would queue through the night for a good spot, and there would be stalls selling food and drink for the spectators.

180 It is estimated that as many as 70,000 people were executed during the reign of Henry VIII.

181 Catherine Howard was so determined to die a queen that she had the executioner's block sent to her cell in the Tower so that she could practice laying her head on it in the correct manner.

182 Some historians have speculated that Catherine Howard's execution, in part, persuaded Elizabeth I to remain unmarried, as she apparently equated marriage with death; understandable, really!

183

Catherine Parr, Henry VIII's sixth and final wife, was twice-widowed by the time she came to marry the king.

184

Catherine was in love with Thomas Seymour, brother of Edward and Jane Seymour, but when the king asked to marry her she wasn't in a position to refuse.

185 The printing press wasn't new by Tudor times, but books were mainly for the well-off.

186 Parr was also the only one of Henry's wives to publish a book. In fact, she was the first English queen to achieve this feat.

187 Not long after Henry and Catherine Parr married, Nicolaus Copernicus (pictured) published his groundbreaking idea that the earth was simply another planet in orbit around the sun (and not the centre of the universe, as had been previously believed).

188 Henry VIII's son Edward was briefly engaged to Mary Stewart, the newborn Queen of Scots.

189 Scottish king James V (pictured) stood his uncle Henry VIII up when they were due to meet on the king's Northern progress.

190 Catherine Parr's story had something of a happy ending after Henry VIII died: she finally married her sweetheart Thomas Seymour (pictured opposite) ...

191

...only to die in childbirth not long afterwards.

192

The girl she gave birth to – Mary Seymour – seems, according to some historians, to have vanished from the records entirely after the age of two, when she most likely died.

193

Catherine Parr nearly met the same grisly fate as Henry's other wives. A warrant was drawn up for her arrest on the grounds that she was a heretic: luckily, however, the warrant was dropped and found by one of her staff, giving her sufficient time to build a decent defence against the charges.

194

Henry's most famous ship, the *Mary Rose*, sank in 1545, three years after his marriage to Catherine Parr, as it was sailing out of Portsmouth. Around 700 men went down with it.

195

By the end of his reign Henry had put on so much weight that his chest measured 53in and his waist 52in – more than enough to make him morbidly obese by modern standards.

196

In fact, Henry was so big by the end of his reign that special devices had to be constructed to winch him in and out of bed, up and down stairs, and on and off his poor horses.

197

Henry VIII's coffin apparently burst open during one of the stops on its way to Windsor, and a dog allegedly licked the blood seeping from the corpse.

198

Despite the famous rhyme that says, 'Divorced, beheaded, died; divorced, beheaded, survived,' the real survivor of the six wives is Anne of Cleves, who lived for almost eighteen years after her divorce from the king – a lady of leisure owning, amongst other properties, Anne Boleyn's old home of Hever Castle.

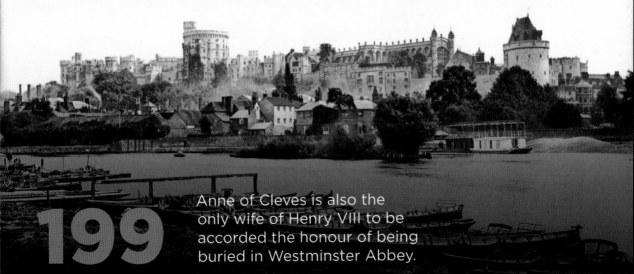

199

Anne of Cleves is also the only wife of Henry VIII to be accorded the honour of being buried in Westminster Abbey.

200

Perhaps the most famous person to play Anne of Cleves is the singer Joss Stone, who had to wear extra make-up to hide her nose piercing and also her tattoos.

201 One of the properties Anne of Cleves received on her divorce, Anne of Cleves' House in Lewes, East Sussex, was never even visited by its new owner!

202 Near the end of Henry's reign one Anne Askew was put on the rack in the Tower of London for preaching 'extreme' Protestant views: she was the only woman ever put on the rack, and was so badly injured that she had to be carried to her execution on a chair.

203 Mercifully, a bag of gunpowder was tied around Anne Askew's neck at her execution: it basically blew her to pieces before she suffered too greatly from the flames.

204 Henry's most famous fool, Will Somers, died in 1560, outliving the king by thirteen years.

205 Money was paid to look after Somers following Henry's death. One probable modern explanation is that he had learning difficulties of some kind.

206 Henry VIII's previous fool, 'Patch', had once belonged to Cardinal Wolsey. Following the Cardinal's downfall, he had to be carried to his new position as Henry's fool in a state of some distress.

207 Likewise, one of Henry's longest-lived courtiers, the Duke of Norfolk (pictured), also outlived the king: he was actually awaiting execution in the Tower of London at the time of the king's death.

208

The Duke of Norfolk was uncle to two of Henry's queens: Anne Boleyn and Catherine Howard.

209 Charles Laughton (pictured) played Henry twice on screen, and was the definitive king for a generation of film-goers.

210 Despite the way Charles Laughton tossed half-chewed chicken legs around his table with abandon, the real Henry was a fastidious eater who preferred to eat in his private apartments and used a finger bowl during meals.

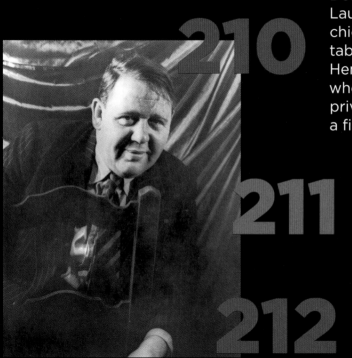

211 Henry's reign is so well remembered it has even been immortalised in one of the 'Carry On' films, *Carry on Henry* (1971).

212 Henry VIII was only fifty-five years old when he died.

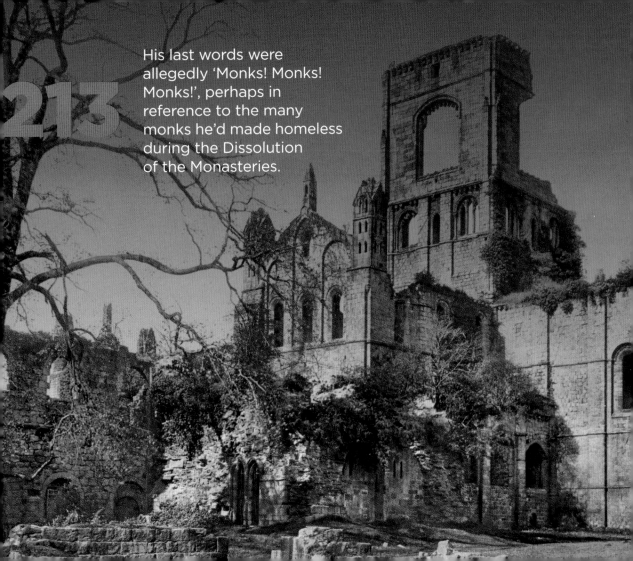

213

His last words were allegedly 'Monks! Monks! Monks!', perhaps in reference to the many monks he'd made homeless during the Dissolution of the Monasteries.

214 Henry VIII's reign lasted for nearly thirty-eight years.

215 Henry VIII almost certainly didn't die from syphilis, as has been rumoured: there are no records of mercury treatment, which would have caused his teeth to fall out; nor was there any record of his nose all but dissolving, a classic sign of advanced syphilis.

216 Anne Stanhope, wife of Edward Seymour, got into a massive row with the widowed Catherine Parr after Henry VIII died; Anne felt that, as the wife of the Lord Protector, the royal jewels really ought to belong to her.

217 Anne Stanhope was apparently a formidable woman. However, the depiction of her as a bed-hopping bawd, as seen in *The Tudors*, is not founded on historical evidence, such as it is.

CHAPTER
THREE

Edward VI

218 Edward VI was just nine years old when he came to the throne.

219 Elizabeth I and Edward were so fond of each other they collapsed into each other's arms on hearing the news of their father's death.

220 The young Edward VI had a whipping boy: this was a boy paid to take the punishment of the actual child who had been bad, a privilege only wealthy families could afford; it was a painful way to make a living!

221

Edward was the star of Mark Twain's 1881 novel *The Prince and the Pauper*, about a young urchin boy who swaps places with the boy-king.

222

Mary Tudor carried on worshipping as a Catholic in private during her brother's reign, despite demands from the Privy Council that she cease and desist.

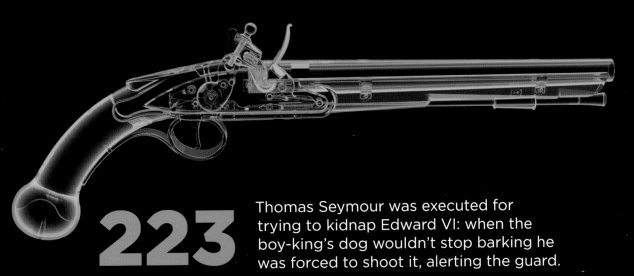

223 Thomas Seymour was executed for trying to kidnap Edward VI: when the boy-king's dog wouldn't stop barking he was forced to shoot it, alerting the guard.

224 Edward Seymour eventually went the same way as his brother, his nephew the king coldly recording the fact in his diary: 'Today, the Duke of Somerset had his head cut off on Tower Hill.'

225 In 1552 two children were killed whilst watching archery practice in Lincolnshire and at a hammer-throwing competition in Dorset: health and safety had a long way to come in Tudor times...

226

A few years later Henry Pert of Welbeck was killed when his arrow stuck in his longbow: when he looked down the shaft, the arrow shot up into his head and killed him!

227

Edward VI was bald at the time of his death, a result of his last illness. Victorian grave-hunters at Westminster Abbey later confirmed this.

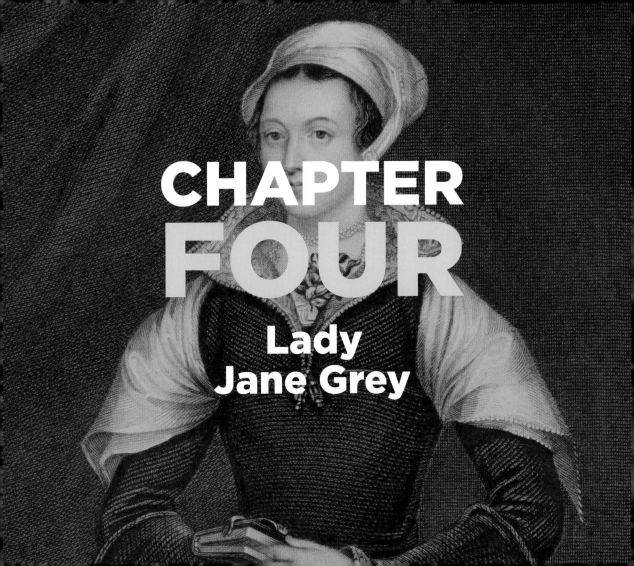

CHAPTER FOUR

Lady Jane Grey

228

Jane was just over sixteen years old when she came to the throne, although the exact date of her birth is open to some dispute, being either late in 1537 or even a year earlier.

229

Famously known as 'the nine days queen', Lady Jane Grey's reign was exactly that – and she didn't leave the Tower of London for the entirety of it.

230 In fact, she didn't leave the Tower of London, full-stop: after Mary Tudor's forces took the ascendancy she was simply imprisoned there until she was executed, having been first blindfolded and then famously fumbling for the block, much to the delight of many a later portrait painter.

231 At the time when Lady Jane was queen, the Tower of London had a menagerie, with lions and other exotic beasts on display.

232 Helena Bonham Carter played Jane Grey in the rather plodding *Lady Jane* in 1986.

233 Elizabeth Bowes-Lyon, the Queen Mother (pictured centre right), is descended from the marriage of Edward Seymour (the Lord Protector's son) and Lady Catherine Grey.

234 Lady Jane Grey had an extremely strict upbringing, complaining at the time: 'when I am in the presence either of father or mother, whether I speak, keep silence, sit, stand or go, eat, drink, be merry or sad, be sewing, playing, dancing, or doing anything else, I must do it ... even so perfectly as God made the world; or else I am so sharply taunted, so cruelly threatened, yea presently sometimes with pinches, nips and bobs and other ways (which I will not name for the honour I bear them) ... that I think myself in hell.'

235 After Jane's execution, her mother was pardoned: her family continued to live at the court of Mary I.

236 However, Jane's sister Catherine incurred Elizabeth I's wrath for marrying Edward Seymour, 1st Earl of Hertford. Both were sent to the Tower, and Edward was fined £15,000 for 'seducing a virgin of the blood royal'.

237 Lady Jane Grey's other sister Mary, small and apparently hunchbacked, also incurred Elizabeth's wrath for marrying without permission, even though the man she chose was not of noble blood at all.

CHAPTER
FIVE
'Bloody' Mary

238 Mary I was England's first real queen regnant, discounting Matilda centuries before, and Jane Grey's brief, abortive reign.

239 Mary was thirty-seven years old when she came to the throne.

240 Mary I burnt almost 300 people at the stake for heresy.

241 During burnings, sympathetic spectators would often hurl more wood on to the flames, making the victims burn faster.

242

However, on a windy or wet day a burning could take ages: if the kindling was soggy, or if the wind blew the flames away from the victim, the agony was much prolonged.

243

Catholic Mary I had the help
of Bishop Edmund Bonner,
who was henceforth known
as 'Bonner the Burner'.

244 Perhaps the worst of all the burnings was that of Perotine Massey from Guernsey in the Channel Islands, who was pregnant and gave birth whilst being burned alive. The baby was then cast into the fire as well.

245 Mary's half-sister Elizabeth pretended to turn to Catholicism to avoid being put on the pyre and managed to fake a stomach ache every time she was expected to attend Mass. Needless to say, Mary soon became suspicious...

246 Elizabeth's view on religion was this: 'There is but one Lord, Jesus Christ. All else is a dispute over trifles.'

247 The young Elizabeth was sent to the Tower of London for her suspected part in a plot to oust Mary, fearing for her life on a daily basis until she was released and placed under house arrest at Woodstock.

248 Woodstock, Queen Elizabeth's prison, was destroyed in the English Civil Wars, but its stones were later used to build Blenheim Palace.

249

Not everyone in Tudor times was called 'Mary', 'Elizabeth' or 'Catherine': there were Barbaras, Graces, Mauds, Amelias, and Honours, among others.

250

Women were thought to be far more sexually ravenous than men in Tudor times, and were to be married off as soon as possible to avoid them going crazy from unfulfilled desire. Mary's marriage – she was in her late thirties – was unusually late.

251

Henry VIII wasn't the only one to be blindsided by the Tudor equivalent of online dating: when Phillip II (pictured) arrived from Spain to marry Mary he was rather shocked to discover that his bride-to-be was a dumpy, prematurely aged and passionately pious woman of almost forty.

252

Mary was also eleven years older than Phillip, making him her Tudor toyboy.

253 The xenophobic English greeted Mary I's husband and his Spanish retinue with a volley of snowballs.

254 Phillip II proposed to Elizabeth I after Mary I's death as a way of keeping England under his control.

255 Mary found conceiving difficult and suffered several phantom pregnancies, keeping the entire country on tenterhooks.

256

Mary never had her sister's gift-of-the-gab, and would stare blankly at those members of the public brave enough to engage her in conversation.

257

The Scottish Protestant preacher John Knox (pictured) thought that any woman, but especially Mary, was unfit to rule. He published a tract on 'The first blast of the trumpet against the monstrous regiment of women' in 1558 as a protest against her reign.

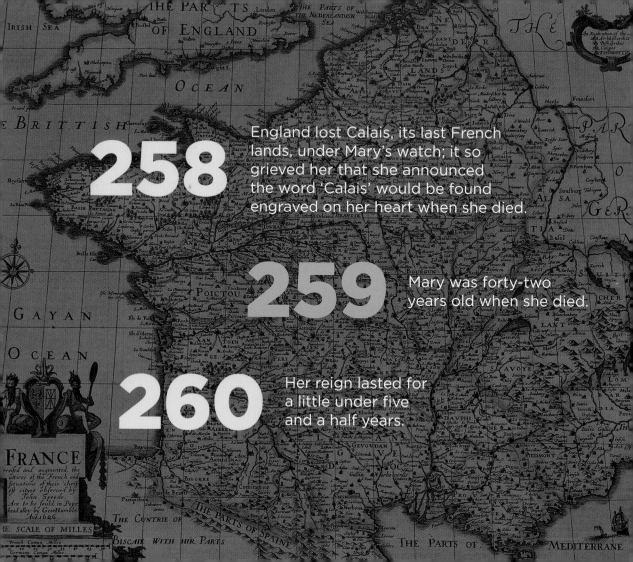

258 England lost Calais, its last French lands, under Mary's watch; it so grieved her that she announced the word 'Calais' would be found engraved on her heart when she died.

259 Mary was forty-two years old when she died.

260 Her reign lasted for a little under five and a half years.

CHAPTER SIX

Elizabeth I

261

262

263

Elizabeth was twenty-five years old when she came to the throne.

The oak tree at Hatfield Palace that Elizabeth was allegedly sitting under when she was told that she had become queen was put in the gift shop for a short time before it deteriorated: now a new tree has been planted on the site of the original one.

Thomas Seymour, despite being married to Catherine Parr, had a thing for young Elizabeth; in the early days of his dalliance Catherine Parr often joined in the horseplay, on one occasion even holding Elizabeth down while Seymour cut the dress the little girl was wearing to pieces.

264

Thomas Seymour would also walk into the young Elizabeth's bedroom in the morning in his nightgown and slap her on the buttocks. To stave off his behaviour, Elizabeth would either pretend to be asleep or make sure she was already up and at her studies.

265

People said
Elizabeth was a
'handsome' woman;
this was Tudor tact
for no breathtaking
beauty (unlike
her cousin, Mary
Queen of Scots).

266

It took Elizabeth's
ladies around
two hours each
morning to get their
mistress ready.

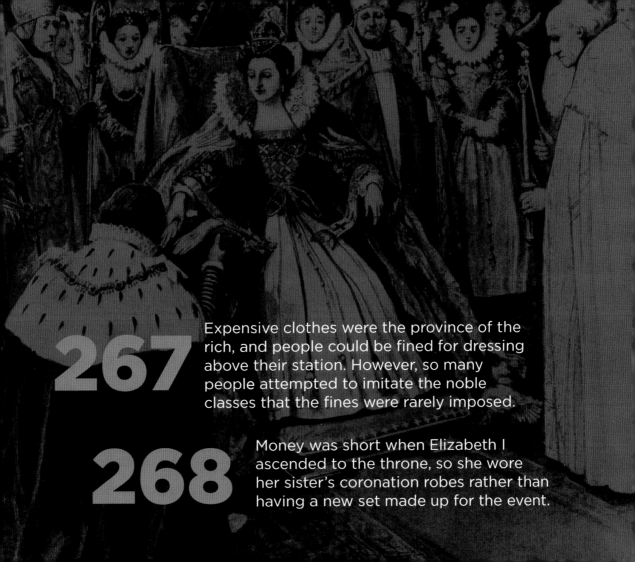

267 Expensive clothes were the province of the rich, and people could be fined for dressing above their station. However, so many people attempted to imitate the noble classes that the fines were rarely imposed.

268 Money was short when Elizabeth I ascended to the throne, so she wore her sister's coronation robes rather than having a new set made up for the event.

269

Dresses came without sleeves during Tudor times. Sleeves were fixed on separately by pins and could thus be swapped around, giving a greater variety of looks from just a few outfits.

270

On one occasion Elizabeth became so jealous of a gown worn by one of her ladies, Lady Mary Howard, that she told her she couldn't wear it, and then proceeded to take it for herself.

271

Elizabeth I could be quite violent to her ladies-in-waiting, and on one occasion she even broke one of their fingers during a domestic dispute.

272

After her death Elizabeth was found to have left approximately 3,000 different dresses.

273 Elizabeth I's face was scarred by smallpox.

274 Rival Mary Queen of Scots also caught the dreaded disease, but her famous peaches-and-cream complexion was saved.

275 The mixture of white lead and vinegar – ceruse – which Elizabeth wore to cover her scars and enhance her pallid complexion was totally toxic to the skin, so heaven knows what she looked like without her face on.

276 Both Elizabeth and Mary Queen of Scots used a variety of wigs and hairpieces – called 'periwigs' – which were carried around in special little bags.

277 In Tudor times a good hairdresser was called a 'busker'; Mary Queen of Scots' lady-in-waiting Mary Seton was said to be an expert busker.

278 Shoulder-length hair was the fashion in Tudor times. When Mary Queen of Scots fled to England she cropped hers down to the scalp in order to avoid being recognised.

279 As well as cutting hair, barber-surgeons also treated wounds and acted as dentists.

280 Bad breath wasn't as big a problem in Tudor times as one might think: people cleaned their teeth with little cloths and also used toothpicks.

281 Elizabeth I thought that the pain of toothache was beneath her royal body. Eventually one of her courtiers offered to have his own decayed tooth pulled out in front of her to demonstrate that the ministrations of a dentist weren't so bad. Nevertheless, in later life she was famous for her rows of black and crooked teeth.

282

Some women actually used to blacken their teeth on purpose: sugar was expensive, and therefore black and rotten teeth were a sign that you had money.

283

However, Mary Queen of Scots was almost floored by her husband Darnley's bad breath. Then again, he did have syphilis: the resulting mercury treatment had caused all his teeth to fall out, with continual drooling one of the main side effects.

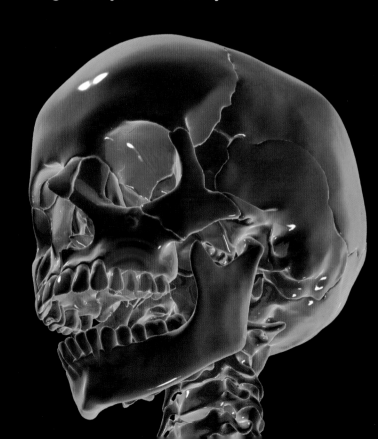

284

Bathing also wasn't such a big deal: the waters and the vapours the body was exposed to during immersion were considered unhealthy, so people bathed as little as possible and covered up the resulting body odours with perfume.

285

Only bathing in waters that were considered pure was thought to be beneficial: the waters at Buxton were one such source, used by Mary Queen of Scots as well as William Cecil (pictured) and Robert Dudley.

286

The Earl of Shrewsbury had a house built at Buxton especially for Mary Queen of Scots so that she could take the waters; today it is the oldest hotel in England.

287

Mary was an expensive prisoner to keep: in order to preserve her complexion she was prone to washing her face with white wine; some sources say she even bathed in it.

288 The original Globe Theatre was also built in Elizabeth's reign, in 1599.

289 No women were allowed to perform in theatres during the great Elizabethan age of plays, so men had to do their best by playing all the parts.

290 Usually women's roles in the theatre were reserved for boys who were barely past puberty, who might therefore be beardless – or, as the Tudors preferred to call it, 'lady-faced'.

291 Shakespeare's *Henry VIII*, which ended with Elizabeth's birth, has in modern times been re-imagined as a Japanese-style Manga graphic novel.

292

In 1600, the actor and dancer William Kempe undertook what came to be known as his 'nine days wonder': he Morris danced all the way from London to Norwich!

293

Elizabeth I was an ardent fan of bear-baiting.

294

Bear-baitings were just one of the ways the Tudors used animals for entertainment in ways we would now consider cruel. There were also cockfights, for which special pits were built (called cockpits).

295

One of the more unusual deaths in Tudor times occurred when Agnes Owen of Hertfordshire was killed in her bed by a bear that had escaped from a bear-baiting pit.

296

Regarding a more modern sport, one of the earliest recorded football games was played at Carlisle Castle in 1568: it was a match between members of Mary Queen of Scots' entourage and those of her English gaolers.

297

Early football was far more violent than the game we know today: injuries were common and deaths possible.

298

Some of the earliest footballs were made from pig bladders.

299 Belief in witchcraft and sorcery was common in Tudor times. Despite several Witchcraft Acts, Elizabeth frequently turned to her favourite astrologer, Dr John Dee, who lived in a house in Mortlake in Richmond.

300 Dr Dee was thought to converse with angels.

301 The first Witchcraft Act was introduced in 1542. Contrary to popular belief, Anne Boleyn was never officially charged with being a witch.

302

Old Mother Shipton – real name Ursula Southeil – was a Tudor woman who made a series of prophecies, published eighty years after her death. She is said to have predicted the invention of cars and planes, and the outbreak of the French Revolution.

303

Another revolution Mother Shipton was said to have predicted was in fashion – the general adoption of trousers by women.

ROBERTVS DVDLIVS COMES LEYCESTRIA BARO DENBIG GVBERN. BELG. VNIT.

Droict et Loial

Ingenio vafer, arte potens, magnusque favore
Principis, incertam liquit post funera famam

304

One of the first court appointments Elizabeth made was for her beloved Robert Dudley to become her master-of-the-horse.

305

Elizabeth herself was the master of the snappy soundbite. On her romance with Robert Dudley, she declared, 'I will have one mistress here, and no master!'

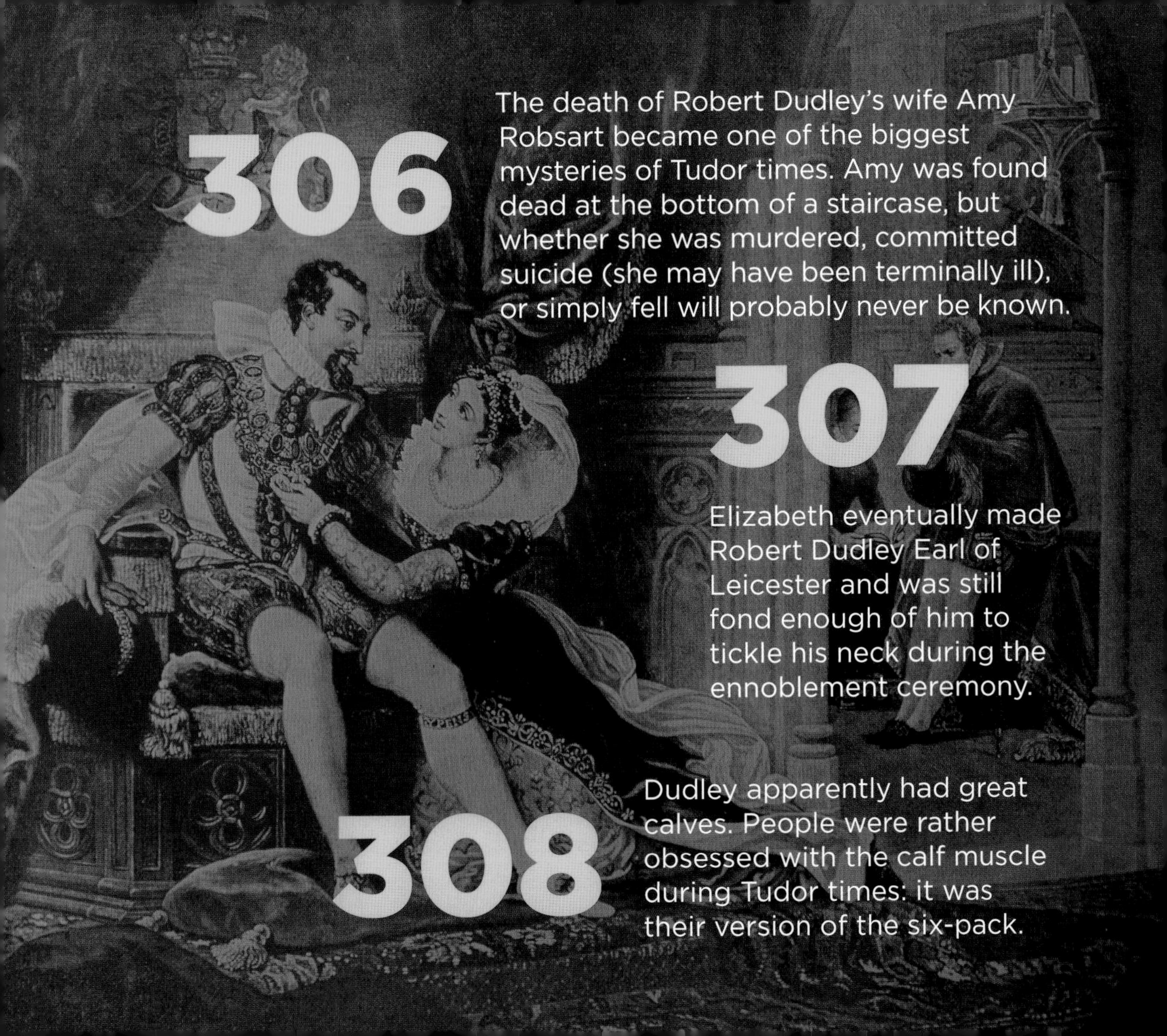

306

The death of Robert Dudley's wife Amy Robsart became one of the biggest mysteries of Tudor times. Amy was found dead at the bottom of a staircase, but whether she was murdered, committed suicide (she may have been terminally ill), or simply fell will probably never be known.

307

Elizabeth eventually made Robert Dudley Earl of Leicester and was still fond enough of him to tickle his neck during the ennoblement ceremony.

308

Dudley apparently had great calves. People were rather obsessed with the calf muscle during Tudor times: it was their version of the six-pack.

309 Sir Walter Scott's famous novel *Kenilworth* is based on the romance between Elizabeth and Dudley, and was set in the castle in which Dudley famously entertained the queen in 1575.

310 Dudley entertained Queen Elizabeth with astonishing firework displays. The original plan was to shoot live dogs out of cannons, but this was called off.

311

Dudley also entertained the queen with plays with elaborate sets, including one with a model Triton riding an 18ft mermaid, not to mention moving islands which carried around the Lady of the Lake and all of her little nymphs.

312

Robert Dudley had a bit of a reputation for being a covert poisoner; when she was a political prisoner in England he suggested that Mary Queen of Scots might be poisoned, but the offer was politely refused.

313

Robert Dudley was also offered as a prospective groom to Mary Queen of Scots. She declined.

TOXIC

314

Elizabeth and Mary Queen of Scots never actually met.

315

When Elizabeth was crowned, the Queen of Scots was declared the true queen of England by her French father-in-law, Henry II, much to the English queen's annoyance.

316

Queen Elizabeth once asked Mary Queen of Scots' ambassador James Melville who was better looking: he tactfully replied that Elizabeth was the fairest queen in England, whilst Mary was the fairest queen in Scotland.

317

Queen Elizabeth then asked who was taller: when told Mary was taller, Elizabeth declared her to be too tall, 'as she herself was the perfect height, being neither too tall nor too small'.

318

Speaking of small, Elizabeth had a dwarf called Tomasen at her court; she appears to have been a cross between a lady-in-waiting and a curiosity.

319

Finally, Elizabeth demanded to know who was the better musician, and the next day had Melville 'accidentally' stumble upon her playing the virginals.

320

Elizabeth briefly considered marrying the French Duke of Anjou. In response, the pamphleteer John Stubbs wrote a tract protesting against the match. For that he had his hand struck off and the stump cauterised; before he passed out he picked up the hand, held it up, and cried out, 'Here is the hand of a true Englishman!'

321

Elizabeth's council were always hopeful that she might one day have children, and as a result all of her 'cycles' were carefully monitored: her washerwomen were bribed to disclose details of the royal bedsheets, among other things.

322 The greatest peril for Tudor women was childbirth, and infant mortality was perilously high. This was why some Tudor families had several sons or daughters with the same name: when the elder one died, the newborn would be given the same name.

323 Newborn babies were tightly wrapped, bound up in a kind of straightjacket; this was to keep their limbs growing straight and was called swaddling.

324 When Mary Queen of Scots went into labour with her son James I of England there weren't any epidurals available, so a spell was cast on one of her ladies-in-waiting to try and transfer the pains to her. It didn't work.

325 After giving birth, women had to be 'churched', i.e cleansed, by a simple ceremony before they could return to their daily lives.

326 In 1566, Mary Queen of Scots' secretary David Rizzio was dragged from her supper room in Holyrood Palace and effectively hacked to pieces. The spot where his body was dumped is marked today with a generous dabbing of fake blood and a golden plaque underneath his portrait.

327 Mary may have had a hand in the planning of her second husband's assassination by gunpowder ...

328 ... as she later married the chief suspect in the murder: the Earl of Bothwell.

329 Bothwell kidnapped Mary and took her to his castle at Dunbar, where it was alleged he 'ravished' (assaulted) her. However, the kidnapping may have been contrived so that Mary could marry Bothwell with no blame to herself, as victims of sexual assault were often wedded to their attackers to restore their honour

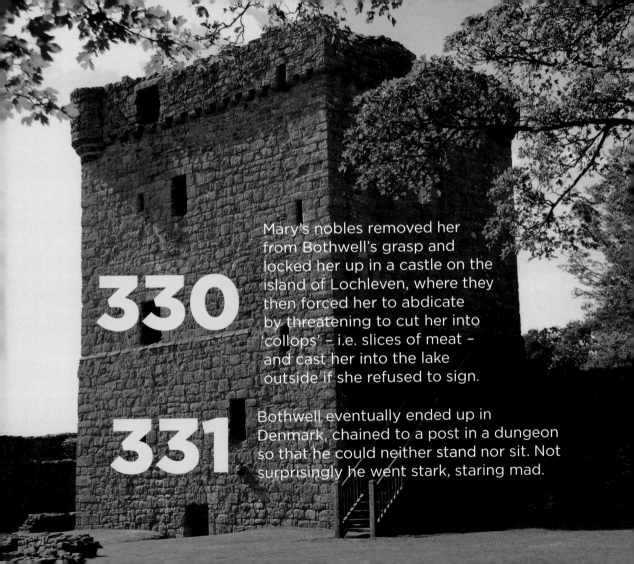

330

Mary's nobles removed her from Bothwell's grasp and locked her up in a castle on the island of Lochleven, where they then forced her to abdicate by threatening to cut her into 'collops' – i.e. slices of meat – and cast her into the lake outside if she refused to sign.

331

Bothwell eventually ended up in Denmark, chained to a post in a dungeon so that he could neither stand nor sit. Not surprisingly he went stark, staring mad.

332 Mary eventually managed to escape from Lochleven, thanks to the help of two smitten young men who managed to get half the island drunk and swipe the keys to the gates with a handkerchief.

333 One of these smitten young men knocked the bottoms from all the boats but one, allowing Mary Queen of Scots to escape.

334 Mary Queen of Scots was almost killed by an earthquake whilst she was in Sheffield Castle: half her belongings disappeared through the hole in the floor that the tremor had opened up.

335

Elizabeth was a notorious miser: when the imprisoned Mary sent her gifts she replied that 'people of my age take with both hands but give only with one finger'.

336

When the Babington Plot, supposedly orchestrated by Mary Queen of Scots to depose Elizabeth, was discovered, Elizabeth ordered that the plotters suffer an even worse punishment than the usual hanging, drawing, and quartering; not too much detail is available of what additional torments they suffered, other than that at one point they were run through with what appear to have been pitchforks...

337
Queen Elizabeth's councillors had a good line in snappy soundbites, like their mistress: regarding the execution of the Queen of Scots, they advised that 'a dead woman bites not!'

338
Spin isn't something confined purely to modern politics: Sir Francis Walsingham, Elizabeth's chief spymaster, concocted a fake plot about Mary Queen of Scots having escaped and enemy ships being sighted in order to scare Elizabeth into signing Mary's death warrant.

339
Mary Queen of Scots' last words, before beginning her prayers, were to her executioner. She said, 'she had never had such grooms before to make her unready, nor to put off her clothes before such a company.'

340
Bull, the executioner of Mary Queen of Scots, botched the job rather badly: first he missed her neck and struck the back of her head...

341 After successfully completing the execution, Bull then lifted up Mary Queen of Scots' severed head, at which point said head fell from beneath the wig Mary had been wearing, leaving him with just her wig in his hands.

342 Finally, Mary's dog appeared from beneath her skirts and ran to the severed head, which had rolled some small distance away from her body, and began to whine piteously.

343 The gravedigger at Peterborough Cathedral was so old that he not only buried Mary Queen of Scots but also Catherine of Aragon: she had died in 1536, some fifty-one years previously!

344 Suntans weren't exactly fashionable in Tudor times: having a tan meant you worked outdoors and suggested you were poor; having white skin meant you were rich. No one was whiter than Elizabeth I.

345 You might think that there were no black people in Tudor England, but this isn't true: there was a black musician in the court of Henry VIII and Catherine of Aragon. Elizabeth also had a young black man in her court whom she referred to as her 'blackamoore boy'.

346 The Tudor period was part of what has been dubbed the 'Little Ice Age', when winters were much harsher than they are now.

347 Winters were so severe that the Thames frequently froze over. 'Frost Fairs' were held, with stalls peddling their wares on the frozen river. One such 'Frost Fair' happened during the early years of Elizabeth's reign.

348

Elizabeth loved having her portrait painted, and the pictures were often full of codes and hidden meanings, of which the Tudors were particular fond. In the 'sieve portrait' she is seen holding a sieve, a symbol of virginity. This harks back to the Roman virgin Tuccia, who, in order to prove her chastity, carried water in a sieve without spilling a drop.

349

The ermine portrait includes a small animal from the stoat family that symbolised royalty.

350

The 'rainbow portrait' (pictured) features Elizabeth wearing a gown covered in eyes and ears, perhaps implying to the onlooker that she sees and hears all in her kingdom.

351

Elizabeth I allegedly thought she was so beautiful that people couldn't look directly at her without being dazzled.

352

The famous 'scandal letter' sent by Mary Queen of Scots said that Elizabeth's ladies laughed at her monstrous vanity behind her back. Luckily, Elizabeth never saw the letter.

353

Bess of Hardwick, Mary Queen of Scots' source for much of the gossip in the 'scandal letter', was the second richest woman in England after Elizabeth.

354

The 'scandal letter' also said that Elizabeth 'wasn't like other women', although quite what Mary Queen of Scots meant has never been satisfactorily explained.

355

When Elizabeth I was a child and displayed in all her glory to visiting ambassadors, no deformity was seen. If the claim in the scandal letter is true, Elizabeth I may have had an unusually thick hymen, or a chromosomal abnormality that led to a lack of ovaries and a shallow vagina.

356

When one of Elizabeth's courtiers, the Earl of Oxford, broke wind in front of the queen, he was so ashamed he left court for seven years. Upon his return, Elizabeth's first words were, 'My lord, I had forgot the fart!'

357

Walsingham House on Seething Lane in London is built on the site where Sir Francis Walsingham, Elizabeth's chief spymaster, worked and died; there is a picture of him in the window above the entrance.

358

Hatton Gardens in London is named after another of Elizabeth's favourites, Sir Christopher Hatton.

359

Sir Christopher built an enormous house to try and impress Elizabeth, but she never even bothered to go and see it.

360 Poor Sir Christopher was also named in the infamous 'scandal letter': Bess of Hardwick told Mary Queen of Scots that Queen Elizabeth couldn't keep her hands off him.

361 Glass was a relatively late addition in many Tudor houses: Hardwick Hall (pictured) – 'more glass than wall' – was not built until the late 1590s.

362 Elizabeth has been featured in *Doctor Who* on more than one occasion; in 2007 she was played by Angela Pleasance, who also played Catherine Howard in the 1970 series *The Six Wives of Henry VIII*.

363 Vanessa Redgrave is one of the few – perhaps the only – actress who can claim to have played both Elizabeth and Mary on the big screen (in *Anonymous* in 2011 and *Mary Queen of Scots* in 1971 respectively). She also played Anne Boleyn in *A Man for all Seasons* (1966).

364

Jean Simmons played Elizabeth in *Young Bess* (1953) opposite none other than her husband Stewart Granger as Thomas Seymour.

365 Bette Davis played Elizabeth twice: in 1939 in *The Private Life of Elizabeth and Essex*, and then again in 1955 with *The Virgin Queen*. Strangely enough, the second film was set some ten to fifteen years before the first.

366 Cate Blanchett has played Elizabeth twice on the big screen, while Glenda Jackson was her generation's screen Elizabeth in the 1970s, also playing her twice.

367 Dame Flora Robson played Elizabeth three times, the third of which was as part of a sketch on *The Morecambe and Wise Show*!

368 One of the strangest people to be cast as the ageing Elizabeth has to be Quentin Crisp, in the movie *Orlando* (1992), based on the book by Virginia Woolf.

369 *Das Herz der Königin* (The Heart of the Queen) was a Nazi war propaganda movie that portrayed Mary Queen of Scots as a fallen heroine at the mercy of the ruthless Elizabeth.

370

The Spanish Armada sailed for England partly to avenge Mary Queen of Scots. It was comprised of up to 130 ships.

371

The wind blew many of the Spanish Armada's ships to their destruction.

372 After the defeat of the Spanish Armada, the Pope declared that Elizabeth I was a formidable foe, and how much better it would be if she were a Catholic!

373 Sir Francis Drake (pictured) completed his famous circumnavigation of the globe during Elizabeth's reign, between 1577 and 1580.

374 Sir Francis Drake may have famously introduced potatoes from New England, but tobacco had already been introduced by the naval commander Sir John Hawkins some twenty-five years earlier.

375 In the 2007 film *Elizabeth: The Golden Age*, many of Drake's achievements were attributed to Sir Walter Raleigh.

376 The colony of Virginia in America was named by Sir Walter Raleigh in honour of his majestic virgin queen.

377 The last 'love' of Elizabeth's life was Robert Devereux, later Earl of Essex; he was thirty-two years her junior, but despite this she was prone to going positively ballistic whenever he looked at another woman.

378 The hot-tempered Essex once drew his sword on Elizabeth after she berated him and threatened to box his ears. Even more amazingly he got away with it and was merely banished from court.

379 Essex committed an even worse faux pas when he barged into Elizabeth's chambers first thing in the morning when she was still undressed, without either face or wig on.

380 The incident had a profound effect on Essex, because he later made reference to Elizabeth I's 'crooked carcass'...

381 The main political rival for Essex was Robert Cecil, son of Sir William; the younger Cecil had a hunchback and as a result Elizabeth called him her 'pygmy'.

382 Elizabeth's motto was *Semper Eadem*, which means 'Ever the Same'.

383 The ageing Elizabeth once had an audience with the French ambassador Sieur de Maisse, during which she wore a dress which bared the entirety of her breasts; she apparently gave the scant material a little tug in order to ensure his attention.

384 However, this wasn't as scandalous as it sounds: showing an ample cleavage was perfectly acceptable for an unmarried woman...

385 ...but not for a married one!

386 As a result of the perils of childbirth, war and disease, the average Tudor life expectancy was only around thirty-five.

387

Despite this, many people lived to a great age, even by today's standards; Bess of Hardwick, lady-in-waiting to Elizabeth I and gaoler to Mary Queen of Scots, was around eighty when she died, and she was far from the exception.

388

Lettice Knollys was one of Elizabeth's biggest rivals. She lived until the amazing age of ninety-one – so much for average Tudor life expectancy, again! – and therefore could claim to have been born in the reign of Henry VIII and to have died in another era entirely, in that of Charles I.

389

In 1601 the Elizabethan Poor Law sent the idle poor to prison, and the 'lame, impotent, old [and] blind' to newly established homes for their care – the beginning of the workhouse system.

390

Elizabeth was so fearful of being seen to grow old that she told older courtiers to stay behind on her later 'progresses': any who could keep up were told to hasten on with her and the rest of the nubile younger courtiers.

391

Elizabeth Tudor didn't die without a fight; in the privacy of her chambers at Richmond Palace she sat propped on cushions for days...

392
...and then stood for upwards of ten hours with her finger in her mouth, in an admirable attempt to stay awake.

393
It was treason to imagine the death of the queen (or king).

394
When Elizabeth's belongings were searched, a ring was found which contained an image of her mother Anne Boleyn, whom she'd rarely referred to throughout her life.

395

James I had an impressive tomb built for Elizabeth in Westminster Abbey, but he made sure that the tomb he built for his mother Mary Queen of Scots was much bigger and grander.

396

Elizabeth also ended up having to share her resting space with her sister 'Bloody' Mary Tudor.

397

However, that's still better than her rival, the Queen of Scots, who in the end had to share her tomb with an extraordinary crowd: Charles I's son Henry and his daughter Mary; James I's son Henry and his daughter Elizabeth (as well as Elizabeth's son Prince Rupert); the eighteen children of Queen Anne; ten children of James II (and also his first wife Anne); and finally, her niece, Arbella Stuart.

398

Elizabeth's corpse was left alone at Richmond Palace where, apparently, 'mean persons' had access to it: quite what they did with it is perhaps best left to the imagination...

399

Elizabeth was sixty-nine years old when she died.

400

Her reign had lasted for almost forty-five years.

Picture Credits

Page 5 Christiaan Lloyd, Shutterstock
Page 6 British Library Flickr
Page 7 Chris Jenner, Shutterstock
Page 8 Christos Georghious, Shutterstock
Page 9 British Library Flickr
Page 10 Georgios Kollidas, Shutterstock
Page 11 Everett Historical, Shutterstock
Page 12 Natsmith1, Shutterstock
Page 13 Library of Congress, LC-USZ62-52608
Page 14 natrot, Shutterstock
Page 15 Cienpies Design, Shutterstock
Page 16 Gail Johnson, Shutterstock
Page 18 thailoei92, Shutterstock
Page 20 Library of Congress, LC-DIG-ppmsc-08580
Page 21. Georgios Kollidas, Shutterstock
Page 22 Jaroslaw Grudzinski, Shutterstock
Page 23 Sponner, Shutterstock
Page 24 Morphart Creation, Shutterstock
Page 25 Georgios Kollidas, Shutterstock
Page 28 Everett Historical, Shutterstock
Page 29 Biomedical, Shutterstock
Page 30 Vladimir Arndt, Shutterstock
Page 31 Library of Congress, LC-DIG-ppmsc-09080
Page 32 mamanamsai, Shutterstock
Page 33 Ariy, Shutterstock
Page 35 EGOR_21, Shutterstock
Page 36 Library of Congress, LC-DIG-ppmsc-08765
Page 39 Library of Congress, LC-DIG-ppmsc-08585
Page 40 Library of Congress, LC-DIG-ppmsc-08570
Page 41 Library of Congress, LC-USZ62-5702
Page 42 Eric2x, Shutterstock
Page 44 tsik, Shutterstock
Page 45 jeep2499, Shutterstock
Page 46 Library of Congress, LC-USZ62-128486
Page 47 agsandrew, Shutterstock
Page 48 Everett Historical, Shutterstock
Page 49 Larysa Ray, Shutterstock
Page 51 Everett Historical, Shutterstock
Page 52 Jiri Flogel, Shutterstock
Page 53 Library of Congress, LC-DIG-ppmsc-08566
Page 54 Richard Melichar, Shutterstock
Page 55 Credit St. Nick, Shutterstock
Page 56 Mariusz Szczygiel, Shutterstock
Page 57 Julia Strekoza, Shutterstock
Page 59 Library of Congress, LC-DIG-ppmsc-08598
Page 60 Library of Congress, LC-USZ62-128712
Page 61 British Library Flickr
Page 62 Library of Congress, LC-USZ62-128712
Page 63 Georgios Kollidas, Shutterstock
Page 64 Bertl123, Shutterstock
Page 66 Wellcome Library, London
Page 67 Kalenik Hanna, Shutterstock
Page 68 mamanamsai, Shutterstock
Page 69 chrisdorney, Shutterstock
Page 70 Library of Congress, LC-DIG-ppmsc-09035
Page 71 British Library Flickr
Page 72 serazetdinov, Shutterstock
Page 74 Georgios Kollidas, Shutterstock

Page 75 Anastazzo, Shutterstock

Page 76 British Library Flickr

Page 77 Georgios Kollidas, Shutterstock

Page 78 BasPhoto, Shutterstock

Page 79 Library of Congress, LC-DIG-ppmsc-08597

Page 81 Markus Gann, Shutterstock

Page 83 Georgios Kollidas, Shutterstock

Page 84 Library of Congress, Prints & Photographs Division, Carl Van Vechten Collection, LC-USZ62-131418

Page 85 Library of Congress, LC-DIG-ppmsc-09037

Page 86 whitehoune, Shutterstock

Page 89 Georgios Kollidas, Shutterstock

Page 90 Everett Historical, Shutterstock

Page 91 X-RAY pictures, Shutterstock

Page 92 serazetdinov, Shutterstock

Page 100 British Library Flickr

Page 101 serazetdinov, Shutterstock

Page 103 Library of Congress, LC-USZ62-100317

Page 104 Miriam Doerr, Shutterstock

Page 106 Marzolino, Shutterstock

Page 107 Christiaan Lloyd, Shutterstock

Page 108 Everett Historical, Shutterstock

Page 109 Richard Semik, Shutterstock

Page 110 British Library Flickr

Page 111 Everett Historical, Shutterstock

Page 112 NatBasil, Shutterstock

Page 113 Puwadol Jaturawutthichai, Shutterstock

Page 114 decade3d – anatomy online, Shutterstock

Page 117 Mopic, Shutterstock

Page 118 Georgios Kollidas, Shutterstock

Page 119 Library of Congress, LC-DIG-ppmsc-08295

Page 120 Stocksnapper, Shutterstock

Page 122 Pavel K, Shutterstock

Page 123 AridOcean, Shutterstock

Page 124 Iosw, Shutterstock

Page 125 Everett Collection, Shutterstock

Page 126 British Library Flickr

Page 128 Library of Congress, LC-DIG-ppmsc-08469

Page 129 solarseven, Shutterstock

Page 130 British Library Flickr

Page 131 British Library Flickr

Page 132 Makc, Shutterstock

Page 135 Alaf, Shutterstock

Page 136 Alf Thomas, Shutterstock

Page 137 phipatbig, Shutterstock

Page 140 British Library Flickr

Page 141 British Library Flickr

Page 142 artcalin, Shutterstock

Page 144 serazetdinov, Shutterstock

Page 145 Library of Congress, LC-DIG-ppmsc-08320

Page 146 Shelby Allison, Shutterstock

Page 148 Ian Woolcock, Shutterstock

Page 150 British Library Flickr

Page 153 Library of Congress, LC-USZ72-190

Page 154 Everett Historical, Shutterstock